TALL SHIPS IN TORBAY

£3.00

Cover: Bellerophon in Torbay, 1815

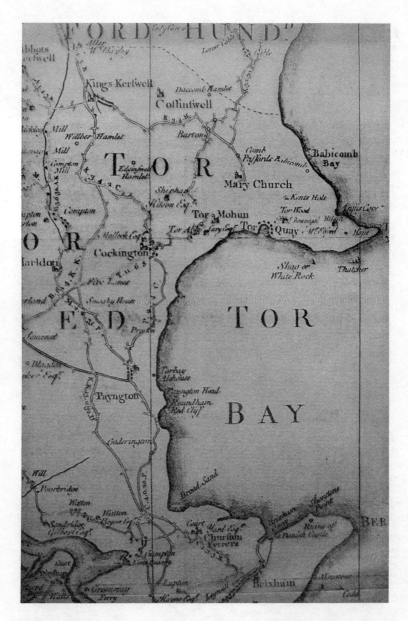

Eighteenth century Torbay; a detail from Down's map, 1765

TALL SHIPS
IN TORBAY

A Brief Maritime History

Best wishes

John Pike

John Pike

Ex Libris Press

First published 1986

Ex Libris Press
1 The Shambles
Bradford on Avon
Wiltshire

Cover by 46 Design, Bradford on Avon
Cover printed by R.A.Blackwell, Bradford on Avon
Typeset in 11 on 13 point Plantin
by Saxon Printing Ltd., Derby
Printed in Great Britain by A. Wheaton & Co. Ltd, Exeter

ISBN 0 948578 03 3

Dedication
To my friends the Coastguards of Brixham. They and their predecessors have safeguarded the mariners in Torbay for over a century and a half.

Note on the Illustrations
The illustrations have been gathered together over many years from various sources but principally from Devon Library Services and Torquay Museum. The source of each illustration, where known, is given after its respective caption; the initials TL are used for Torquay Library and TNHS for Torquay Natural History Society. The assistance of both is acknowledged with sincere thanks.

CONTENTS

Author's note
This book is a narrative account based on a chronology and source list which appeared in the *Devon Historian* No. 29: October, 1984. It has always been the writer's policy to produce work which hopefully will encourage his readers to research further on their own. The bibliography therefore includes all the important books and pamphlets. The references at the end of the book list these briefly by the author's name; additional sources consulted being recorded fully.
J.R.P.

Introduction

Historians invariably view events at sea through landlubbers' eyes - as if standing on a high cliff, gazing towards a distant horizon, pen in hand. For many of the seamen and travellers whose stories are told here, looking towards the shore from the deck of a ship was the last sight of their native land. There are no accounts of their feelings and only a few from newcomers. One visitor briefly in Torbay remarked in his native French: *Enfin, c'est un beau pays* - At last, that is a beautiful country. Napoleon was soon on his way to St.Helena.

George Medlicott Goodridge, returning from a real-life Robinson Crusoe experience in the South Seas, waited in high anticipation "for some conveyance to land. I was in sight of my native village - my heart beat high. The venerable church of Paignton was in full view, and with my glass I could trace well-remembered objects, even the very dwelling of my childhood and the home of my parents." Not long before, home was far away as he lay in one built of stones and wood, sea-elephant skins covering the roof and seal-skins serving as sheets, blankets and counterpanes.

Perhaps it is appropriate that the most eulogistic introduction to Torbay should come from a work of fiction. Nevil Shute, one of the most popular mid-century novelists, summed it up in *Lonely Road*:

> In front of us the confines of the bay were visible, the flat land rising up into tall cliffs at the north end. There were hills there and a wonderful town upon the hills that followed the slopes down to the tideway; a magic town built of high harbour walls and shining palaces beside the sea. All this was half-shrouded in mist; in the bright sun it was shot with colours gold and blue -
>
> Like a flight of rose leaves fluttering in a mist
> Of opal, and ruby and pearl and amethyst.

Livermead with fishing vessel in about 1830 (TNHS)

Torquay about 1840 (Lithograph - TNHS)

I   FROM ROMAN TIMES TO THE REIGN OF HENRY VIII

In the Beginning ....

When Neanderthal man found refuge in Kents Cavern from the cold of the last Ice Age many thousands of years ago Torbay (though of course it was not recorded as so named until the fourteenth century) was dry land. The rivers of northern Europe flowed across a plain (the English Channel) to a coastline now many metres below the waters of the Atlantic Ocean. When the earth became warmer, the ice-sheets which had covered vast areas began to melt and recede towards the Pole. Sea levels rose and between the eighth and sixth millennia BC Britain became isolated from the continent of Europe. A coastline was formed as the lowest parts of the land were gradually engulfed by the rising waters. Torbay had probably been thickly forested for 2,000 years or more when this took place. There is some confirmatory evidence of this in stumps of trees which have been uncovered off Torre Abbey sands and at Goodrington on rare occasions when tides have been exceptionally low. Leland, the Elizabethan traveller, referred to again later, commented on their existence when he was on the shores of the Bay in the sixteenth century.

Much nearer our own time, though still 2,000 years ago, the Romans invaded southern Britain and their vessels were constantly at sea during the 350 year occupation. Ptolemy's *Geography, Book II* suggests that they had a haven and landing-place at Axmouth in East Devon near the terminus of the Fosse Way. As south Devon was within sight across Lyme Bay it is reasonable to assume that they knew all about Torbay as well and, indeed, had some sort of military camp on Berry Head. Scattered finds of coins and pottery are said to confirm this.[1]

TALL SHIPS IN TORBAY

The arrival of the Saxons in Devon during the seventh or eighth centuries AD has been widely chronicled although there is at present no firm evidence of their being in Torbay. The early arrivals would have come by sea as well as land and so the smooth, sandy beaches of Torbay would have provided ideal landing-places. The final conquest of Devon by them was rapid and apparently achieved with little opposition.[2] They were essentially people who cultivated the land; whether of not they were fishermen too can only be guessed at but catching fish for food certainly dates back to prehistoric times. What is certain is that, when the Premonstratensian monks settled at Torre Abbey 300 years later, fish was part of their daily diet and most of it was caught in the Bay.

There were, however, much more warlike invaders between the Saxons and the Normans. The Danes came to the east of England in the early ninth century and in 851 they came as far west as Devon. There has been much speculation that the Danish hordes who were beaten by Coerl and his men of Devon at Wicganbeorg had come ashore on the Torbay beaches and that the battleground was at Weekaborough near Paignton. The *Anglo-Saxon Chronicle* is clear concerning the name but exactly where Wicganbeorg was located is less certain. In 997 and again in 1001 the marauding Danes were once more off the Devon coast: they sailed up the Teign and landed to pillage and destroy. It is possible, of course, that their longships came inshore and that fires burned in Torbay as well, but the sparse records that have survived reveal nothing. It is a fact that the early settlements which later grew into the villages of Paignton, Cockington and St Marychurch are a mile or so inland rather than being beside the sea as might be expected; perhaps this was because the watchers on the coast needed the time to hasten back home to warn of impending attack.

The arrival of the Normans in England after the Battle of Hastings in 1066 had little effect on local people for more than a lifetime. The manors and lands passed into the possession of new owners, but for the indigenous population, oppression and serfdom continued unchanged as labour was mostly wanted on the land. The establishment of Torre Abbey on the western side of the Bay probably brought some social changes as the monks, by teaching and example, and with the support of their lay-brothers, encouraged the development of a number of trades including fishing. The foundation charter[3] of William Briewera granted them the "right to fish and trawl in the bay". The Charter was followed by a further agreement in 1327/8 between the Abbey and James de Cokyntone which confirmed fishing rights in the neighbouring manor of Levermede (Livermead). The monks were also given authority to spread and dry their nets below the cliff on Cockington land. Here is proof that the fishing industry has been established in Torbay for 800 years or longer.

In 1338 a charter was granted in favour of the Black Prince by which the waters of Dartmouth became his property and he gained the right to levy dues on all trade within the port. This included "Brickesham, Peynton, Kingswere and Toteneys". Torbay remained within the "Port of Dartmouth" for several centuries. These rights later became the property of the Duchy of Cornwall which leased it in 1659 to the town of Dartmouth for 200 years. The linking of Torbay with this ancient town means that, although much documentary evidence has survived, it is often difficult to abstract the relevant items. Contemporary records, for example, show that Dartmouth provided 31 ships and 757 men for the siege of Calais in 1347; these must have included vessels from Torbay.[4]

There are few early references to commerce and voyages to other countries. However, it is noted that dues were demanded at the rate of 6d. in the pound on all tin taken out of the port.

Transport of pilgrims to the Tomb of St James of Compostella in north-west Spain was established during the century and the Devon ports were among the earliest in the business.[5] At first only Plymouth and Dartmouth were involved but the Patent Rolls show that Teignmouth and Brixham took part at intervals as well; for example, John Marshall of Brixham was granted a licence to convey 60 pilgrims. Five hundred years later small passenger vessels for "day-trippers" are still controlled by law and the number of passengers permitted on board included in the licence; occasionally owners are prosecuted for exceeding its terms and conditions. Progress and time do not affect the operation of the law.

After the death of Henry V in 1422 the Regency which followed sold off the Navy by public auction.[6] Subsequently ships were impressed for the transport of troops and supplies in time of war. About the time John

Marshall was sailing out of the Bay with his pilgrims, other ships of the port were being requisitioned for that purpose. It was not until the end of the century that Henry VII was hiring the transports and merchant-men he needed, so ending impressment of ships about 1500. However, the "pressing" of men continued for several centuries.

Early Torbay Merchantmen
Thanks to the efforts of an anonymous person something is known about commercial activities in Torbay some 500 years ago. He transcribed pages from the *Account Books of the Custom House Officers of Dartmouth*. The first of these concerns vessels trading in and out of the Bay just about the time when Christopher Columbus was making his voyages to discover the New World (1499 - 1500).[7] For the reason already given it is not possible to say exactly where the cargoes were loaded but there is no doubt from where the vessels originated. They included the *George* of Torre "whereof John Bartelot is master"; the *Trinity* of Torre (John Cokman, master) and the *Mighell* of Torre (John Selle, master). Seven vessels from Brixham and three from Paignton were listed on many occasions, the *Cristofer* of Paignton, the *Trinitie* of Brixham and the *Mary* of Paynton among others. Cargoes on which duties were paid included: lasts of herrings (last = 12 barrels), pieces of Devonshire tin, wine, silk and "barrels of pitch and rosen".

In 1513 Henry VIII was at war with France and among the 39 ships requisitioned was the *Mary* of Bryxham with a crew of 99 men and captained by Richard Calthorpe. She was described as being "80 (later on 120) tons"[8] and was probably used as a transport; a month's payment for her use was £38.11s.8d.

The problems caused by an undefended Torbay were recognised about this time when in 1522 a letter from the Earl of Surrey to the King noted:

> The only danger (to Dartmouth) is that if an enemy were to land at Torbay, only two miles from where the ships ride [in the River Dart], they may cast fire upon them .... To avert this write to the Bishop of Exeter saying you are informed they are making a blockhouse beside Brixham within Torbay and if they would

make another at Churston you would help them with ordnance and powder. I see by the gentlemen who have been aboard today that they would do it at their own cost.

It is plain that even then official support was forthcoming only to *supplement* local enterprise and effort.

A few years later John Leland, chaplain and librarian to the King, was dispatched around England, ostensibly to gather materials for a history but, according to some authorities, more likely as a spy. One Transcription[9] chronicles thus:

After passing Penton almost three miles there cumethe down a praty broke and running by the shore sands goith in to the sea at Torrebay village and priorie a mile off. There is a peere and socour for fischar boats in the bottom by Torre Prior .... The west pointe of Torrebay is caullid Byri and more than within a mile of this pointe is a praty toune of Fischar men called Brixham and this toune is a member of the privilege of Dertmouth. I marked almost in the middle of this bay one house [Possibly Torbay House at Paignton, demolished in 1874] set on the hard shore and a small peere by it as socour for fischar boats. Fischar men hath at divers tymes taken up with theyre nettes yn Torrebay mussons of harts [antlers of wild deer] whereby men may judge that in tymes past it hath been forest grounds.

Exactly what condition the harbours around Torbay were in at the time of Leland's visit is uncertain. "Torrequay" must have been in a very poor state of repair as chalices and other church-plate were sold in 1540 "for the reparacion of the harbour".[10] Paignton certainly had a proper harbour at Roundham as John Barons was "Kaywarden" there in 1621 and his *Account Book* survives. Some years earlier the Earl of Pembroke's *Survey* (1567) notes: ".... land lying at Rowneham, which they hold for the convenience of fishermen as a market for the sale of fish ...." Much later but sometime before 1800 it had become a ruin, being recognised then only as a "creek" but still called "Paignton Pier from the remains of an old pier which formerly existed there". Brixham probably had the best haven under the sheltering limestone of Berry

Head. Isolated references in the *State Papers* tend to confirm this; for example in 1534 a licence was granted to John Cherrington, merchant of "Excetter" allowing him to import 200 tuns of wine (a tun of wine was 252 gallons) "and unlade the same at Brixham."

Old Torquay Harbour in 1804; view from the west (TNHS)

It is however from another extract from the *Custom House Books*[11] that the clearest picture of seaborne trade at this time can be obtained. The period covered is 1538-39, just about the time the great monastic institutions including Torre Abbey were being disbanded and their assets scattered. The names of the vessels had changed little: the *George* of Torre, the *Mary* of Bryxham and the *Leonard* of Paignton still appeared; new ones included the *Jhesus* of Torre "whereof John Leche is master". He is listed later as master of the *Savyor* of Torre and paid duty on "5 hoggsheads of pilchards, valued at 33s.4d. consigned by William Huchmore and eight more worth 53s.4d. .... by William Mowre." Incoming and outgoing cargoes were now very much more diverse. As well as wine and tin and many "pilcharddes" the manifests

14

included salt, allmontes (almonds), corrupt wine (this appears also as *vini egre*) and barrels of fruit.

In the sixteenth century the woollen cloth industry was thriving again in Devon. Kerseys, a coarse woollen, was being woven at Totnes and elsewhere. Naturally these went out through the port of Dartmouth. A half-cloth was carried in the cargo of the *Mare* of Torre while the *Marke* of Brixham (John Wallter, master) carried 40 cloths to an unknown destination. (A Devonshire cloth of assize was 24 yards long and 2 yards wide). On 12th.August 1539 the *Peter* of Torre, with Richard Waymouthe as master sailed outward with a varied cargo of 15 dozen calf-skins, 21 cloths and 45 dozen tanned calf-skins. The name of Waymouthe in this sea-faring connection is of special interest as the family has been continuously resident as tenant-farmers in Cockington and St Marychurch since the fifteenth century and possibly earlier.

The last of the published extracts relates to the years 1618-19.[12] By then the pirates were in Torbay and most of those trading were Dartmouth ships. There were large consignments of Newfoundland fish being re-exported but the local vessels continued to carry on the trade in pilchards. The *Grace of God* (45 tons) took a cargo to Malaga in Spain while the *Hound* of Torbay sailed to St Malo with 38 hogsheads consigned by John Martin of "Cokinton". Nicholas Roope of Dartmouth put aboard the *Laurel* (William White, master) 200 axes, 60 long knives, 400 dozen caniscare knives worth £5, 40 spades, two dozen mattocks and adzes worth 10s., and 43 pounds of white beads worth £2., and consigned to "the Amazons". There is no record that the *Laurel* ever did reach South America but the beads were obviously intended for barter with the native inhabitants.

II   IN THE DAYS OF GOOD QUEEN BESS

The First Pirates

The sixteenth century was a period of wars and the time when English sailors, particularly those from the West Country, were beginning to establish their superiority on the seas of Europe. Until then the Portuguese and Spanish had been the major explorers who had set up the trade routes to Asia and South America. Some of the sea-outlaws of Queen Mary's time were to become the trusted servants of Elizabeth.[1] In 1558 Devon received more licences for privateers than any other English county, a simple way of transferring men from pirate to patriot in time of need. The Acts of the Privy Council contain many references to Torbay over the next decades. In 1573 Thomas Carew, the sheriff of Devon was, with other Knights, ordered to examine the activities of one Predeaux who with other captains was committing acts of piracy on the Devon coast. Carew was ordered to go to Torbay and apprehend them.

The following year two further similar events were recorded. A ship of 60 tons belonging to Peter Heyne of Dantzig was taken and "spoiled at Torbay by John Cole an Englishman". He was also charged with being responsible for taking a ship belonging to "the company of Stilliard." For both he was ordered to be apprehended and to answer at law. Also in 1578 Thomas Ridgway, officially recorded as "of Torbay" but then owner of the manor of Torwood (part of Torquay), was ordered to make a personal appearance before the Privy Council in Westminster on "matters relating to piracy in the county of Devon". In the absence of any further information in other surviving documents it may be that he was being called to account for turning a blind eye to the illegal deeds which were going on nearby.

IN THE DAYS OF GOOD QUEEN BESS

The names of several famous Devon sea-dogs appear in a letter sent to Sir John Gilbert by the Privy Council in 1579. It concerned a Spanish vessel laden with oranges and lemons which had been taken out of Dartmouth and into Torbay by his brother Humphrey. Sir John undertook to see that his brother and "Walter Rawley" remained on shore. It has been explained[2] that Gilbert, Ralegh and some associates had planned to recoup losses with some speedy privateering by seizing the ship. It was however not the moment to upset Spain. The Irish Catholics even then had for years been seeking help against the English from the courts of France and Spain and from Rome. James Fitz-maurice, cousin of the Earl of Desmond, had the support of the Pope and ships in Spain ready to sail. Although they did not menace the coast on this occasion, the comings and goings of privateers and pirates must have excited the local inhabitants. The Armada when it did come up the Channel 30 years later bringing the damaged *Nuestra Senora del Rosario* to anchor must have seemed to them just one incident in an ongoing adventure.

In the 1560s privateers were commissioned by the Prince de Condé; soon the Catholic Netherlands followed their example and they too sent out privateers, the "Dunkirkers" who plagued the Devon coast for nearly a century. Torbay provided shelter and probably stores - from which no doubt the Brixham traders profited the most. The Dutch in Torbay were reported to "suffer no man to pass them unspoil'd". In 1576 there were 13 of their privateers lying in the Bay and the Privy Council instructed the Vice-Admiral to seize them - but only if he could do so without shedding blood.

At present there are no known accounts of what was happening to the several hundred people living in the local villages at that time. One can only conjecture that the men were called upon to ferry food and water to the ships and possibly to become unwilling crew members as well. Whilst there is no hint anywhere of acts of repression it is obvious that these seamen fathered children of Torbay women.

The National Archives do however reveal the picture of life ashore among the resident gentry. In 1579 for example, a letter was sent to the Sheriff, Vice Admiral, Justices of the Peace, and others requiring them to:

> make diligent enquiries of all piracies by seas and robberies by land committed by such persons and heretofor pretended to accompany Sir Humphrey Gilbert, Walter Rawley, Fortescue and others in their voyages and commit them to prison .... Those disordered persons [had] made their abode commonly in the roads of Torbay and having committed many piracies bring their spoils to land. All justices, but principally Mr.Cary of Cockington, to have diligent care of the safety of the ships which repair thither, and for the removal of pirates [and] the apprehension of them when they come to land.

The naming of Mr Cary in this way implies that the Privy Council did not feel that he, like his neighbour Thomas Ridgway, was acting in the Queen's interest as decisively as he should have been - leniency towards the pirates was very common in Elizabethan England.

In 1583 Sir Humphrey Gilbert performed a major service for his country when he secured the island of Newfoundland. Present day maps show "Torbay" just north of St John's while on the mainland of Nova Scotia Torbay (some seven miles across) is protected by Berry Head on its southern side.

The official rupture of relations between England and Spain took place just two years later and trade became prohibited between Protestant England and the Catholic countries of Europe. Local fishermen were soon in desperate straits as there had been a substantial export of fish from Torbay to France and Italy for many years. A petition was sent on 21st October 1585 to the Justices of the County praying them to secure from the Privy Council "a licence to transport fish .... notwithstanding the restraint." The reply, which took four years to arrive, permitted the export of fish but not to Spain or Portugal or "to any port not under the King of France".

As has already been expressed the passage of the Armada from west to east was just one occurrence in a continuing encroachment by outsiders. Once this episode was over the defensive forces drafted in to deal with it continued to be stationed around the Bay; some four years later in 1592 there was a quarrel between the two local Deputy Lieutenants, Sir George Cary of Cockington and Sir John Gilbert of Greenway.[3] Each had to raise and command a regiment, the men coming from the Hundreds of Haytor, Coleridge and Stanborough (that is most of South Devon). Gilbert deliberately "poached" some of his from Sir George's "tenants and neighbours so that he [Cary] has to go twenty miles or more for recruits". The ill-feeling continued for some time: at one stage Sir John Gilbert had to remind the Council that when the Spaniards were about he brought a thousand men to Torbay but "that then George Cary [a Catholic] lay quiet". Nevertheless in 1599 Cary was formally named as the Commander of all the forces around Torbay.

Towards the end of Elizabeth's reign both the North Sea and the English Channel were thick with Dunkirkers.[4] In October 1600 "five Dunkirkers are on the coast; one rides at anchor in Torbay. They interfere with the shipping." Their exploits may be judged by a declaration made in May 1603 that "8 Dunkirkers have carried off a Portuguese prize taken by me and left him in Torquay Harbour". There is no evidence that Sir George Cary was given any instructions as to how he should deal with them or indeed with any of the pirates who must have joined them at anchor.

The Privy Council received petitions and demands for better protection, particularly from Exeter and Dartmouth. The vacillations of governments and leaders change little over the centuries: at first the owners were criticised for not arming their ships properly and combining together for self-protection; then there was the promise to send men-of-war to drive off the pirates: finally the Council ordered that the masters who refused to put to sea should be committed to prison. The question must of course be asked: where were the English privateers so prominent only a few years earlier, who had done the work of the Queen's ships? The answer was that they had gone further afield in search of "prizes" and had left home waters largely undefended. English seamen were about to experience the miseries which they had been inflicting on others for nearly a century.

Spanish Ship in Torbay 1588[5]

Over the centuries sightseers have gathered on shore many times but on at least five occasions they were witnessing, not just a gathering of ships but also, if they had known it, major events in the history of Britain. The first of these was the arrival in Torbay at the end of July 1588 of the crippled Spanish Armada vessel the *Nuestra Senora del Rosario* with her foremast down and her rigging a tangled heap on the deck as she limped to anchor under the menacing guns of her captor.

The Spanish Ship in Torbay, 1588 (Illustrated London News engraving, 1873)

The events which led up to the dispatch of great fleets of ships from Spain need little explanation here. King Philip of Spain was determined to overthrow the Protestant Queen Elizabeth, and to achieve this a vast army had been assembled at Dunkirk. Tension however had been building up for some time and, just as in later centuries when danger threatened, preparations for defence had been made all along the south coast in the usual English fashion - on a tight and ungenerous budget.

During the autumn and winter of 1587 the country was put in as good a state of readiness as time and the finances at the Treasury had permitted. Special attention was paid to the coastlines of both Devon and Cornwall as it was most likely the assault would be made somewhere along the south-western peninsula. Indeed, it had been said that Torbay was earmarked as one of the three or four possible landing-places because of its lack of any defences. Earlier in Henry VIII's time the Earl of Surrey had warned how easy it would be for an army to land and then attack the Fleet lying in the Dart "with fire". As a result, the building of bulwarks was authorised at Brixham, among other places, but there has always been some doubt about the work actually done. Just above the Berry Head Hotel and hidden by trees and shrubs which have grown up in the last hundred years is the Castle or Round Top Battery and which might possibly date from this time. Guns sited there would have commanded a good range of fire over the Bay right up to Napoleonic times. Alternatively there could have been something built above Overgang of which all traces have vanished.

In the spring of 1588 defensive forces on land were strengthened too. Devon was organised into three military divisions; each was authorised to raise two regiments with eight hundred men and a smaller number of horses. In south Devon the two appointed to command were Sir Edward Seymour of Torre Abbey and George Cary, then owner of Cockington. This must have been considered an important task as Mr Cary was recalled from Dover where he had been directing the building of defensive works. It was obviously not easy creating a force of this size locally. In August 1587 the Privy Council suggested that "150 men of Mr.Fulford's band [they had been raised in the interior of Devon] ought to be assigned to Mr Cary for the better defence of Torbay." Sir William Courtenay and Sir Thomas Denys were recruiting (poaching may be the more appropriate word) south Devon men so that the unfortunate Mr Cary "he that dwelleth upon the sea coast of Torbay, a place of most danger, is neither able to raise his number as other colonels do, nor [has he] any one band to back him upon any occasion of service."

The other Deputy Lord Lieutenant locally was Sir John Gilbert who had recently built a new residence on the banks of the Dart (Greenway House, very much later the home of Agatha Christie). He is believed to have had a thousand or more men and only had to ride a mile or two to the flat land at Galmpton Warborough when his men were assembled. This trained force was a sixteenth century Home Guard, and like them would have been vastly outnumbered if the enemy had ever landed.

There were 132 ships in the Spanish fleet which had "3,165 pieces of ordnance" between them. They had on board 8,766 sailors, 2,088 galley slaves and 21,855 soldiers and volunteers. As this was a holy crusade there were 300 monks and priests as well. The Devonshire ships were mustered at Dartmouth and comprised: the *Roebuck*; the *Phoenix* "Mr. Gawen Champernown's bark of 70 tons which carries 70 men"; Sir John Gilbert's *Gabriel* "burthen 120 tons with 80 men"; Mr Adrian Gilbert's *Elizabeth* and the *Samaritane* of Dartmouth. Some idea of the cost to the Queen's Treasury can be gleaned from surviving documents: the Captains each received £3.5s. and the men 10 shillings each for their month's service. Of these ships by far the largest was the *Roebuck* being 350 tons; she was owned by Sir Walter Ralegh and "commanded by a most daring Captain, Jacob Whitton".

As soon as the Spanish fleet was sighted in the Channel, beacon fires were ignited all along the coast. The nearest one to Torbay was at Beacon Hill near Marldon (where the television mast now stands). Others were lighted on Berry Head, on Warberry Hill by the men of St Marychurch and on Torre Hill by the men of Tormohun. Further fires to the east spread the general alarm.

The *Nuestra Senora del Rosario* was the flagship of the Andalusian squadron; in command on board was Don Pedro de Valdez and it was he who surrendered the ship to Sir Francis Drake after it had been damaged in a collision with the *Santa Catalina* and then engaged by Hawkins and Frobisher. Drake's very name brought fear to the Spanish noblemen but it was Captain Whitton who towed the great vessel into Torbay with the help of some Brixham fishermen. Almost immediately there were letters to and from the Privy Council in London. As the Armada passed up-Channel there was "a bloody skirmish off Portland" but the English ships were forced to break off the engagement because their ammunition was exhausted. Small fast pinnaces had been sent immediately to scour the coast for fresh supplies. The arrival of this rich prize in Torbay was a godsend and so the first communications concerned the removal and transfer to the English fleet of all the gunpowder and shot found.

This done Sir John Gilbert and Cary wrote: "Have taken the Spanish prisoners, about 400 soldiers out of the Spanish ship at Torbay and brought them ashore and now request what to do with them. The charge of keeping them is great and the peril greater." The ruthlessness of the Inquisition was well known and the Spaniards were a hated enemy. There were clearly fears that the local people might start a massacre, which is probably why the landings on Torre Abbey Sands were delayed until the Militia was mustered and the demi-lances brought from neighbouring St Marychurch. There is on record that an order existed which authorised the execution of all Spaniards "wherever they may be found"; fortunately this does not seem to have been contemplated on this occasion.

The 397 prisoners were accommodated in the Spanish Court according to a later document; this was of course the former monastic tithe-barn which has been known ever since as the Spanish Barn. This medieval building then probably had an upper floor (the timbers were finally removed only about 50 years ago) so would have been dry and quite roomy. There is nothing to tell how the prisoners fared while at Torre Abbey. Various legends have sprung up over the centuries: one of a Spanish nun who is said to walk the avenues on cold and moonless nights; another of a young maid who, unwilling to be parted from her lover, donned male attire and joined the Spanish army with him. The truth however is probably more prosaic. There is evidence, supported by finds of bones at various times, that at least a few succombed during their incarceration and were buried in front of the Barn (now a pitch-and-putt golf course).

The State Papers record how Sir Edward Seymour was compensated for "cumbering his house" with a gift of four pipes (about 105 gallons) of wine which had been taken from the ship.

Almost immediately there were conflicting claims as to who had captured the vessel. A petition was drawn up and presented to the "Lords of the Council" which under seven headings attempted to justify the rights of the commanders of the *Margerat and John* to some of the spoils. It is not clear whether they received satisfaction in the end but one matter did come to light during the interrogation of Don Pedro in London. Drake admitted that he had taken 3000 pistolets in coin (a pistolet was an old Spanish coin worth today about 80 pence) from the ship but declared, as a reason for the plunder "that he had not three pounds left in the world". Undeniably an alternative explanation of "sailing near the wind".

The *Rosario* lay in Torbay for nearly four weeks with a skeleton crew on board. This term takes on ominous undertones when viewed with reports made by the two Deputies later in a second letter to the Privy Council:

> .... the rest, which are 166, for the ease of our country from the watching and guarding of them, and conveying of their provisions of their victuals unto them, which is very burdensome unto our people in this time of harvest. We have therefore placed them aboard the Spanish ship to live upon such victuals as do remain in the said ship, which is very little and bad, their fish unsavoury, and their bread full of worms, and of small a quantity as will suffice them but a very small time.

After some partial repairs the ship was taken around to the Dart. There "a true inventory" was made which shows particularly what massive armaments were then available; they included cannon pedros, basilicos and culverings - one of the latter is recorded as weighing 4,700 hundredweight. These remained in their places but "the small ordinances lest they should be embezzled away" were carried ashore. Contemporary costs can be obtained from some of the items in "the Book of Charges":

	£	s	d
Wages of 50 men after the rate 10/- a month for a man	25	0	0
Eight boats to tow the ship about from Torbay to Dartmouth	1	6	0
Carpenters to set up a Jewery Mast (jurymast) in Torbay		8	4
Guarding and watching the Spaniards two days and nights and one day at their landing	1	10	0

Once in the Dart further stores were disposed of and there was a serious estrangement between Cary and Gilbert. The former accused Sir John of "not taking any pains where no profit ariseth" - he was refusing to pay his share of the cost of maintaining the prisoners as instructed thus leaving the whole burden on Cary's shoulders. On the other hand he was forcing "106 of the said Spanish prisoners remaining a-ship board hard by his house at Greenway to every day hardly labour in his garden in the levelling of his grounds."

As far as Torbay is concerned this was not quite the end of the affair. Mr Cary seems to have had some sympathy for the prisoners; he refused to accept the promise of the Privy Council that they would eventually pay the 2d. or 3d. daily allowance, but went to Exeter, and after taking advice, to relieve their misery "advanced the money himself other they must have perished".

Newfoundland Fisheries

The Torbay men obviously played their part in developing the lucrative trade in cod which lasted several centuries, although the numbers who went out from each port are difficult to ascertain.[6] Dartmouth was much involved[7] but there are few references indeed to the Bay towns. However in one document dated 1635 there was a petition[8] from over 800 Newfoundlandmen, "masters, owners of shipping and seafaring inhabitants from St Marychurch, Tormohun, Paignton, Brixham, Churston and Stoke Gabriel." If this number is correct it shows the scale of local participation. The petition concerned tithes and other duties they were unwilling to pay but there were soon greater worries about the "bye-fishermen" who sold their catches to "sac" ships.[9] The former were men who either travelled out each year or were resident in Newfoundland and who employed boatmen on a wage basis. The "sac ships", some owned by wealthy London merchants, did no fishing at all but simply loaded catches for a swift voyage back across the Atlantic. Wage-earners were unwelcome, as owners and crew traditionally shared both profits and losses. As is explained in a later chapter, Brixham fishermen today are still "share-fishermen".

Two unusual trades were practised locally. Tanned and tarred aprons were made for Newfoundland fishermen at Dartmouth and there was a thriving industry making fish-hooks at Ogwell. Both have long since died out.[10]

III TROUBLEMAKERS FROM NORTH AFRICA AND EUROPE

John Nutt and the Seventeenth Century Pirates

The seventeenth century, like the sixteenth, continued to bring ships of all types and nationalities into the Bay. The Dunkirkers, with both Englishmen and Scotsmen in their crews, made trouble all along the coast; their vessels were fast and well-armed - ordinary merchantmen could not outrun them and even warships could not catch up with them when they were carrying full sail.[1] There were, however, other more vicious visitors: the corsairs from the Mediterranean, sometimes also referred to as the Moorish pirates or the Sallee Rovers.

The decline of Spanish sea-power had opened the way for the Moslem states of North Africa to encourage pirates on a large scale: some had the help of English renegades as well as those from other nations. They certainly anchored in Torbay, from where they sailed out to molest ships in the Channel and to harry the fishing vessels returning from Newfoundland.[2] Their most nefarious activity was the carrying off of local people to slavery in large numbers. The records at Dartmouth tell how scores of men were taken, while in Cornwall 60 men, women and children were taken straight from a church into captivity. In 1618-19 the Privy Council were aware that about 300 ships had been forcibly removed to Moroccan and Tunisian ports. In 1625 there were petitions to London from the wives of some 2,000 West Country sailors pleading for their ransom or rescue. The Salleemen, when forced into south Devon ports in bad weather, threw their prisoners overboard and pretended to be honest captains of a friendly power.

Again the question must be asked: where was the Navy during this difficult time? After James I made peace with Spain in 1603 the Navy was badly neglected - the few ships in commission were stationed in the Thames; the south coast was virtually unprotected.

There was a third brand of troublemaker in the Bay carrying on what may be termed "piracy proper" which "harassed the government and the merchant".[3] Peace with Spain had put many privateersmen out of business. They had no desire for the quiet life and so became sea-going pirates in the Mediterranean or caused havoc in home waters.

There were many letters between Dartmouth and London in the 1620s.[4] The Mayor pleaded: "Dunkirkers are so thick about Torbay, and also pirates of our own natives, since the peace with France, that no ship can pass free." In 1631 "four pirates, once in four or five days, make Torbay their rendezvous and do much mischief." In the same year "Donne the pirate" was in Torbay.

The most notorious of these named pirates was John Nutt of Lympstone who, it appears, was so happy in Torbay that he had his family with him. Nutt was originally a gunner on a Dartmouth ship and is said to have acquired his pirate vessels by capture off the coast of Newfoundland. He obtained his crews by offering good and regular pay, something the Navy of the day could not do. After attacking ships in both Irish waters and the Western Approaches he set up a retreat at Torbay which was so strongly defended he was immune from capture. He, like others similarly placed, was in the position "to buy a pardon" which would enable him to retire with his profits. This brought him into conflict with Sir John Eliot, who had been appointed Vice Admiral of Devon in 1622.[5] His patent from the Lord Admiral permitted him to act as his deputy on maritime matters. He collected dues from wrecks and was also charged with applying the new statutes, which included the suppression of piracy. His emolument (payment) was an agreed part of the proceeds from all prizes, wrecks and other fees which he shared with the Lord Admiral.

Eliot arrived in Torbay and, by subterfuge with a pardon which proved to be a false one, enticed Nutt ashore and to surrender. John Nutt was at once arrested and his ships seized. He was then taken triumphantly to London. Within a month Sir John himself was being held in custody in the Marchelsea Prison while Nutt walked free in the city. He had rendered a service to the King's Secretary Calvert by protecting the new colony of Newfoundland and thus in return a blind eye was turned in high places. After claims and counter claims Nutt and his associates were granted "pardon of all depredations and piracies committed before June 25th last, with right to retain all their ships and goods except those taken piratically since May 1st which are to be restored to their owners." The Privy Council was also told that "Captain Nutt deplores his former practices." Eliot was released and later became one of the great Parliamentarians of the century. In spite of promises Nutt quickly reverted to his old ways: soon afterwards a Mayor in Ireland was asking for help against "the incursions of John Nutt the pirate."

The effect of the operations of all these predators on local life can only be guessed at. The situation was further complicated nationally when after the accession of Charles I, it was resolved to fight a new naval war against Spain. It started in 1625 and to meet the Navy's needs an Order was issued in April that "250 men be pressed in Devon". This was for a great fleet about to be assembled at Plymouth.[6] The expedition to Cadiz (where the attack was repulsed with heavy losses) was poorly equipped, the men diseased and mutinous from the outset. Matters were even worse when it returned. During 1626 there was a serious outbreak of a virulent disease in the port, possibly typhus or the plague. Thousands died and for some time captains were refused permission to disembark their sick and dying men. Some, most likely penniless and starving, were allowed into south Devon because in January the Mayor reported "Soldiers home from the war [are] billeted in Dartmouth." This undoubtedly caused the disease to spread into the district; he wrote again later: "The inhabitants still forsake the town though the plague has ceased".

The English fleet was back in "Torbay the fittest place" on 23rd September. Ten days later it was still there "much in need of cordage and sails". Admiral Lord Willoughby was forced to discharge some vessels because they were "leaky" and "others were becoming unserviceable daily." It does however appear that the Navy's presence kept the pirates away.

In 1627 war against France broke out once more; Charles I found funds by, among other things, pawning the Crown Jewels. To save money the maritime counties were required to provide ships ready for sea and English privateers were authorised to come into being again. Between 24th June 1625 and 14th August 1628 *Letters of Marque or Commissions to take Pirates* were granted to over 930 vessels by the Lord Admiral. Of these three came from Torquay (not Torbay): the *Prudence* of Torquay (80 tons), *Providence* (90 tons) and the *Benjamin* (35 tons) both owned by Henry and James Barnes. One-tenth of the value of all prizes taken was to be handed over but it is obvious from contemporary correspondence that some captains were not doing so. The *Oxford English Dictionary*'s definition of "letters of marque" in this context is of great interest:

> .... this became practically a licence to fit out an armed vessel and employ it in the capture of merchant shipping belonging to the enemy's subjects; the holder being called a privateer or corsair and entitled by international law to commit against a hostile nation acts which would otherwise have been condemned as piracy.

Thus Torquay had for a time privateers of its very own at sea. Meanwhile conditions on naval ships continued to be deplorable and morale remained at a low ebb for the next 30 years.

Dutch in Command of the Channel
The decline of the Navy after about 1630 meant that the piratical fraternity and the ships of enemy nations continued to anchor in the Bay from time to time. Dutchmen and Frenchmen lay wind-bound and "often sent ashore for water and provisions". Nevertheless a defensive fort, its location now unknown, was dismantled, its stone used for lime-burning and its armaments melted down for horse-shoes.[7] The Dunkirkers were still marauding in the Channel: on one occasion they cast off "Frenchmen to the number of one hundred and upward .... were brought into Torbay where they were landed, being left altogether destitute." Six Moors of Sallee "were distressed and forced to land". They unsuccessfully tried to steal a boat. There is no explanation as to why defence works should have been demolished as there were continuing fears that a landing in force would be made. Special

29

instructions were given that the warning beacons be visited daily in case they should be ignited in error and the whole county called out. This little known period in Torbay's maritime history was a turbulent one. Mid-century had still not been reached when the Fleet of the Earl of Warwick anchored on its way to Dartmouth; only two years later Vice-Admiral Batten paused with his ships before helping Fairfax's assault on Dartmouth. The Civil War period generally seems to have affected life in Torbay only a little.

The atmosphere of the times can be judged by a letter sent by Prince Maurice to Colonel Edward Seymour:

> Diverse persons disaffected to His Majesty's service and peace of the kingdom do associate and meet together about Torbay in a hostile and warlike manner to the great terror and distraction of His Majesty's loyal subjects. I authorise you, for the suppression of such insurrection, to repair with your force to Torbay .... there to repress and reform the same, and in the case of opposition or resistance to slay, kill and put to the execution of death by all ways and means all such enemies and traitors and rebels ....

Opponents of the King were to be given short shrift.

In 1660 the Monarchy was restored but Charles II, the new King, soon quarrelled with the Dutch and war was declared yet again in 1665. The Dutch were soon masters of the Channel, and English merchantmen were gathering in the Bay awaiting arrangements for convoy outwards. These included a "Guinea coast" fleet of the recently formed West African Trading Company awaiting escorts in July 1666. The Dutch Navy also anchored in large numbers, sometimes more than 50 vessels at a time and on one occasion the King refused to bring his own ships around from Bristol until they had sailed away.

The French also caused trouble.[8] Captain de la Roche landed a mile from Torquay, marched up to the tiny harbour and commandeered the *Mary* of Ostend which had been scuttled shortly before his arrival. He caulked the holes drilled in her and sailed her off as his "prize". A fortnight later Sir Thomas Allin forced him to yield up his booty "without Demur" after inviting him, and his captains, aboard the *Monmouth* for dinner.

As pointed out earlier the English Navy was in such a parlous state that it was not even fitted out when the Dutch Admiral de Ruyter sailed up the Medway and did much damage there. He then moved down the Channel into Cawsand Bay and, a little later, into Torbay. He was able to anchor without hindrance and, although he did not have sufficient troops to launch an assault on shore, he burned two ships in the harbour and fired a salvo or two in the direction of Torre Abbey; this might almost have been a rehearsal for the landing of William of Orange twenty years later.

One event, although of brief duration, was to have a far-reaching influence on the future prosperity of Torbay: in the summer of 1671 there was a Royal visit, His Majesty with his brother James sailed into the Bay in his yacht, accompanied by others, after a visit to Plymouth. They called at Nethway House where the King is said to have left behind a leather coat. For a time it was exhibited to guests but later the owners were disenchanted with the Merry Monarch so it was cut up "and used for baser purposes."[9] Nevertheless it was the first time that a fleet of pleasure craft had been seen in Torbay and this has been the one activity which has remained virtually unchanged for over three hundred years.

Peace was made with the Dutch in 1674 (the Third Dutch War of 1672-74 was fought in alliance with the French) but the English continued to be harassed by French ships which waited off Berry Head as predators for their prey. There were fortunately no major incidents within the confines of the Bay but there is a document which acknowledges Samuel Pepys' gracious thanks "to Edward Seymour for protecting the Dutch man-of-war against three Frenchmen lying in Torbay" - an example of former enemies being guarded against erstwhile friends. Pepys, now best remembered for his *Diary*, became secretary for the affairs of the Navy in 1673 and was responsible for its recovery after its disastrous decline during the reign of Charles II. By the end of James II's short reign it had been brought to a high point of material efficiency.[10]

The Landing of William, Prince of Orange, 1688

The events which led up to the invitation by a group of English nobles to William, Prince of Orange, an avowed Protestant, to come and claim the throne of England is part of our national history and need not be repeated here. A commentator of the day, clearly a strong opponent of the Catholic King, told his readers that William landed at Brixham "to drive forever the pusillanimous traitor from the shores of England". It is therefore at the moment when the Dutch fleet was in the Channel

The Landing of William, Prince of Orange, 1688 (Engraving of Turner painting - TNHS)

under the command of Admiral Arthur Herbert (later the Earl of Torrington), one of the Englishmen who had gone to Holland as a professional adviser to the Prince. Part of the force should have landed at Dartmouth, the other in Torbay,[11] but in the night, due to the imcompetence of the pilots who misread the bearings of the land, the fleet had passed beyond both places and were off the Start in a rising easterly gale at five in the morning.

A contemporary account[12] quaintly explains "the wind chopping about to the West-ward; upon which we stood fair by Dartmouth and so made for Torbay ...." The same south-westerly prevented the English fleet from stopping him. It continues: "Upon his arrival at Torbay, the People on Land, in great numbers, Welcom'd his Highness with loud Acclamations of Joy".

A fuller account[13] is given by another Englishman, John Whittle, who was a chaplain on one of the ships. He related how they rode at anchor for a while before the Prince "had set his Feet on Land, then came all the Lords and Guards, some going before his Sacred Person and some coming after .... The Navy was like a little City, the Masts appearing like so many Spires ...." The first men ashore were "six regiments of English and Scotch" under the command of General Mackay, with the support of the 18 guns of the *Porpus* which had been ordered to run aground. Neither troops nor armaments were needed as there was no opposition; indeed, a great welcome awaited the Dutch if Mr. Whittle's account is to be fully believed. The "landing of William of Orange", the second great event in Torbay's maritime history was under way.

One of the first tasks of the Prince was to send "Captain M... to search Lady C...'s House at Torre Abbey." Mr Cary was "a very rigid Papist who entertained a Priest in his House" and who, when he saw the white flags flying from some ships' mastheads, assumed it was a French fleet poised to land troops in support of James II: he therefore summoned the whole household together to sing a Te Deum. As soon as it was realised who the visitors were, most ran off, except the Dowager Lady Cary and some of her faithful servants. There was obviously rumour and counter-rumour, one being that several of the Prince's soldiers had been shot and that the house was burnt in retaliation. Whittle declared "that there was nothing in it at all, for our People did not give them one reviling word, nor they us; some lodged there while we were at Torbay."

The Prince himself went up to the high ground above Brixham and marked the place where his army should encamp; then he "returned down the Hill into the Fishermans little Houses: one of which he made his Palace at the time." Horse guards and foot-soldiers commandeered some of the town houses, while "All the Lords were quartered up and down at these Fishermens Houses, whereof these Poor Men were glad." The next three days were taken up landing the future King's Army which totalled "18000 Horse, 3000 Dragouns and 1800 Foot besides 1000 Volunteer Persons of Quality."

It was cold and frosty at night "and therefore sundry Souldiers were sent to fetch some old Hedges and cut down the green Wood to make some Fire." Others went "into the villages thereabouts to buy some fresh Provisions for their Officers, being we were newly come from Sea; but alas! here was little Provision to be gotten. There was a little Alehouse amongst the Fishermens Houses which was so extreamly throng'd and crowded that a Man could not thrust in his Head, nor get Bread or Ale for Money. It was a happy time for the Landlord, who strutted about as if indeed he had been a Lord himself ...."

Brixham Harbour and William of Orange statue erected for bicentenary (TL)

By Wednesday the 7th the Prince was ready and the march started through the lanes past Churston and Paignton to Ford House at Newton Abbot. The journey was not without problems, as "the Lanes hereabout were very narrow, and not used to Wagons, Carts or Coaches, and therefore extream rough and stony which hindred us very much from making any speed ...." The time at sea had also taken its toll for "As we marched here upon good Ground, the Souldiers would stumble and sometimes fall because of a dissiness in their Heads after they had been so long toss'd at Sea, the very Ground seem'd to rowl up and down for some days, according to the manner of the Waves."

William formally became King of England when he accepted the Crown jointly with the deposed monarch's daughter Mary. His problems were still not over as he was forced to go to Ireland, where he soundly defeated James at the Battle of the Boyne on 11th July 1690. It was of course this Protestant victory which symbolised the beginnings of the "Irish problem" which has been with us ever since.

There were soon repercussions in south Devon as well. Admiral de Tourville and the main French battle-fleet sailed into Torbay confidently expecting support from the Jacobites and other opponents of the new régime. This was not forthcoming as the local gentry, with vast numbers of their retainers, flocked to the shore and put up defences at every possible landing place. This is confirmed by a letter from Plymouth dated 31st July 1690 that "Lord Lansdown is this day at Torbay where our militia and others are in arms, consisting of 30,000 cheerfully to oppose them." Although the French had at one stage 160 sail in the Bay they were frustrated from taking any action other than "manning 40 boats and 5 galleys with 400 men" which went out of Torbay to neighbouring Teignmouth where they burnt some small ships and most of the town. "French Street" in Teignmouth is so named in recognition of this disaster. In 1691 the French fleet was again seen off Torbay; the Militia, this time 10,000 strong, was "drawn to the water's edge to prevent them landing." Combined fleets of English and Dutch men-of-war were soon using the Bay, and the "hated French" sailed away for good. As we shall see in a later chapter, French ships continued to be a constant danger to Protestant Britain for another century and more.

Brixham Harbour from Windmill Hill, 1824 (Lithograph by W.Daniell - TNHS)

Brixham Inner Harbour, late 19th century (TL)

Brixham Inner Harbour, late 20th century

IV TORBAY SMUGGLERS AND WRECKERS

The "Gentlemen" at Work

Customs duties date back to the time of Magna Carta when the King by royal prerogative regulated all the commercial activities in his realm. Later sovereigns, including Edward I, passed statutes controlling the goods subject to duties and the amounts to be levied on each. Over the centuries a bureaucracy developed which by 1678 had produced an establishment in each port. At Dartmouth, for example, there were a collector, a surveyor, two waiters and searchers and four boatmen. In addition Brixham, Salcombe and Torquay each had a waiter and searcher, making a total of 11. The position at Torquay was then held by Bonaventure Cowell who received an annual salary of £3.15s.

The imposition of these duties and the consequent desire of local seafaring men to avoid paying them led to the development of smuggling. No doubt smuggling activities went back to the time of the imposition of those duties, but it was after the Smugglers Act of 1736 (which made it a felony to import certain prohibited items) that the illicit "trade" really developed. The high cliffs and sheltered coves with their gently sloping sandy beaches along the south Devon coast were ideal landing places, and soon many hundreds of people, seafarers and landsmen alike, were engaged in bringing ashore cargoes of wines and spirits; there are also records of huge quantities of tea and tobacco being landed.

Soon there were Customs cutters at sea and the *Letters and Orders* books kept in the Customs House at Dartmouth (unfortunately the originals are believed to have been destroyed by enemy action in World War II) give a fascinating insight into the activities of both smugglers and the "Revenue" in the eighteenth and early nineteenth centuries.

Custom House Record, 1678; note old spellings: Bricksham, Saltcombe, Torkey (Library of HM Customs and Excise, London)

They tell the full stories and frequently give the names of those caught red-handed at sea with their illegal stuff. In 1783 there was an encounter between Captain John Swaffin, commander of the shallop *Spider* (a light open boat) "in the King's Service" and a larger smuggling cutter "mounting sixteen carriage guns [and] which has of late used this and the western coast." This vessel had a crew of 50 men who, "with the assistance of Thomas Perkinson, a noted Brixham smuggler", had landed considerable quantities of contraband "on Paignton sands between the hours of 12 and 4." According to Swaffin there were 1,500 casks of spirits and four tons of tea. The scale of operations at this period must have been vast. Some years earlier in 1727 a smuggling vessel was brought into Torbay with a cargo of arrack (a spirit distilled from palms, molasses or rice) and tea. A contemporary account refers to the master as being "the last of the smugglers left here". Far from that being the truth, he must have been one of the first to be caught.

There has always been something romantic about the smuggler.

Defiant to restrictive laws, he is depicted as a dark-jerseyed, full-bodied, silent figure in sea-boots with a keg of brandy on his ample shoulder. The reality was very different: the smugglers ashore worked in groups of 50 or more, and behaved ruthlessly against the Revenue men who dared to oppose them. Officers disappeared over cliff-tops and their men were viciously beaten. Along the coast in east Devon a memorial in stone records how John Harley, Customs House Officer, "fell by some means or other from the top of the cliff to the bottom, by which he was unfortunately killed." A few miles in the other direction on one occasion, the local "gentry" were able to bring their cargoes on to a sheltered beach while their wives "entertained" the local coastguardsmen in their cottages nearby. The ladies of Hope Cove were committed to the Quarter Sessions at Exeter for their parts in the affair. The Station Commander of the coastguard at Brighton had to be equally firm, promulgating a signal for vigilance, "there being reason to believe that an attempt will be made to corrupt our men through the medium of females." One-upmanship by the Torbay smugglers is explained in a poem many verses long concerning "Resurrection Bob" Elliott[1] who was suffering from gout when "a cargo of stingo" was secreted in his cottage. So Bob had to "die" ....

> Then the Commodore said
>   Respect for the dead
> Restrains us from searching the den
>   But we'll keep it in sight
> By day and by night
>   Till they've buried the duffer and then ....

Bob and his friends were forced into evasive action:

> There was no other chance
>   But to lead them a dance
> So a coffin of monstrous size
>   Was made, and good need,
> For Bob was no reed ....

The "spirit" was thus borne away but

That very same night
  A terrible sight
Was beheld by Coastguards three
  On the Totnes road
With a phantom load
  They could solemnly swear t'was he
And each declared
  Bob Elliott glared
Like one whom they would rather not name ....

It was of course not the Devil himself but a very human smuggler who lived to tell the story and pass it on to his children.

While much of this may be fiction, Jack Rattenbury's escapades, on the other hand, were very real. He was the most notorious smuggler in the South West, born at Beer, but operating in Torbay at various times during his adventurous career. A reformed character in later life, he settled down and wrote his autobiography.[2] He recounts one episode in detail. Taken by the Revenue and placed on board a man-of-war, he resolved to escape, and enlisted the support of his wife and her friends. He continues: "As soon as she and the other females were alongside I jumped into the boat .... and called 'Shove off'." The duty crewman fired two shots, the first through the sail, the second hitting an attached rope and causing it to fall down. Hoisting it again the escapers rowed furiously towards Bobs Nose (now better known as Hopes Nose at the north end of the Bay) with a fusillade of shots from the pursuing sailors hitting the water all round the boat. Rattenbury concludes: "I started over hedges, fields and ditches and got to Torquay; and went to a public house kept by a friend where I got dry clothes and refreshments."

The first coastguard station seems to have been at Babbacombe quite near Hopes Nose. There was soon one at Brixham, and it has been recorded that in the 1830s the Chief Officer at Paignton was forced to dismiss "Lieutenant P who released two smugglers without authority and concealing the fact that any men were present when a cart, two horses and 46 tubs were seized ...." This is one of the few known examples of corruption, which is surprising. The life of "revenue men" was hard: some were at sea in all weathers; others trod slippery cliff-paths and faced other dangers of the night for very poor pay.

The first half of the nineteenth century was the heyday of the Torbay smugglers. One writer explained:

> Torbay gradually acquired a reputation for being a place where almost anything in reason could be done without fear of interruption .... The barns of Mr Cary at Torre Abbey and Mr Mallock at Cockington were often packed with smuggled goods; doubtless without the knowledge of those worthy gentlemen but nonetheless to the exceeding profit of some unknown person and the loss to that common enemy - the Revenue![3]

The repeal of legislation in mid-century made the illicit import of tobacco and brandy uneconomic. In more recent times a more insidious trade, that of drug-trafficking, has affected parts of the south coast of England. HM Coastguard and HM Customs, successors to the old Revenue men, need all the sophisticated electronic and other aids they can acquire, to bring these late-twentieth century callous, mercenary smugglers to justice.

The Torbay Wreckers

The Cornish wreckers, thanks to the fictional efforts of Daphne du Maurier and others, have achieved a notoriety which has not been matched in the neighbouring county. It was a common belief that ships were cast up on beaches for the benefit of the inhabitants, and that it was fair, as in love and war, to "assist" vessels in distress by showing lights on exposed headlands. It is perhaps no coincidence that when the first positively identified ship was wrecked in Torbay in 1657, "Captain Pley and constables were recruited to prevent the country people making havoc with her."[4]

The best documented case of wrecking involves the brig *St Peter* driven ashore near Torre Abbey Mansion house in 1771. She was laden with groceries for Exeter, said to be worth £4,000. The *Flying Post* reported:

Immediately on the vessel being dashed to pieces, the Country people came down in great numbers to plunder the wreck and even robbed the Captain of his watch; on which Geo. Cary, Esq., of Tor Abbey, accompanied by his brother, armed several men, and secured the ringleaders, whom they sent immediately on board a man-of-war, and by their endeavours saved all that could be saved of the cargo and secured it in their cellars.

An interesting example of summary justice at the time the press-gang was busy in Torbay.

Lanterns designed to lure vessels on to the beaches at Oddicombe and Babbacombe were hung on the horns of cattle grazing at St Marychurch. Masters were intended to believe that they were rounding Hopes Nose into the shelter of Torquay. While there is printed confirmation of the intention there is no proof the ruse ever worked; no vessels ever seem to have been wrecked on any rocks immediately north of the Bay.

V BUSY TIMES IN TORBAY, 1700–1815

A Strong French Enemy, 1690-1713 The strength of the French was so great that the need was soon realised for a major naval base in the west. In 1691 a Commission was set up to consider the relative merits of the Dart, the Plym and the Tamar for the site of a dockyard capable of building and re-fitting the largest warships of the day.[1] The eastern bank of the Tamar at Point Froward was the chosen location, and the construction commenced of what is now known as Devonport Dockyard. Until the breakwater was built a century later Plymouth Sound offered poor shelter during south-westerly gales, and so the Navy preferred to use Torbay. As well as providing complete safety from the prevailing winds it was deep enough and had good holding ground for the great three-deckers to anchor safely at all times.

Maybe it was this continuing presence which encouraged "Arthur Robinson, Gent.", to print a broadsheet,[2] with map, giving "reasons for making a harbour or mould in Torbay" in 1696. A safe anchorage for 300 sail was envisaged but it was the Navy which would benefit most, preventing:

> the great inconveniences and mischiefs that have happened for want of their victuallers and tenders bringing provision to them when in Torbay, being often detained by contrary winds which have kept them so long that sometimes part if not all of the summer expedition has been much impeded if not lost thereby, besides the hardships and discouragements the poor seamen have laboured under by scarcity of victuals ....

Parliament was unimpressed; perhaps it was not thought necessary, as a letter sent to London the same year reported that "the Royal Fleet rides safe in Torbay, being in no wise terrified by the vast number of French privateers which almost surround them."[3] The French might have been more bold if they had known the true state of affairs: although peace was not signed until September 1697 the State Papers reveal that in July Sir George Rooke had come to Torbay "to be recruited with provisions, which had been very sparingly furnished this year or the Fleet might have been of greater use." A month later the ships were still "lying in Torbay when they might have been at sea." The Frenchman Du Pointy had taken and sacked Cartagena without hindrance, taking home booty valued at £3 million sterling. The country, it was said, was "much vexed by this loss" which was all due to the absence of the English who were anchored in Torbay "for want of provision."

Even during the short periods when there was peace between the two countries and ships moved freely in the Channel, the weather still brought huge concentrations of shipping into the Bay. In 1701 Sir George Rooke was back with a combined English and Dutch fleet numbering over 250.

After the death of William III, Queen Anne declared war on France yet again, and merchantmen were soon gathering at Spithead in great numbers, to be escorted to the Mediterranean and the East and West Indies. In July 1703 one unseasonal south-westerly gale brought in an immense armada for three days. This must have been a spectacular event because as well as hundreds of merchant vessels there were the combined English and Dutch squadrons under Admiral Sir Cloudesley Shovel, nearly 60 heavily-armed warships as well. The object of this expedition was the relief of French Protestants in the Cevennes "who had been goaded into insurrection by the persecution of the Papists."[4] The English battle-line contained many famous ships including *Royal Oak*, *Warspite*, *Association* and the *Torbay* (80 guns and 500 men). The last had, shortly before, distinguished herself by breaking the harbour boom at Vigo and enabling others to destroy or capture 17 of the enemy. In spite of all the fire-power, the rescue mission to France was unsuccessful, and the Fleet was back in England by November.

Rooke's squadron was away on active service which culminated in the capture of Gibraltar in 1704, and their prolonged absence left Torbay open to intruders. In September, help was sought against four French privateers "sailing to and from Torbay, which had hindered the fishing and trading all the summer." This war with France lingered on until 1713.

Just two years later another and quite new enemy appeared in the Bay. On 3rd April 1715 a letter informed London: "This day there came into Torbay five or six Swedish men-of-war." After this brief incursion there followed 40 years of local peace, and people were able to carry on their normal affairs, which undoubtedly included landing illicit cargoes of brandy and tobacco.

Conflict with America and France, 1759-1805

The weakness of Torbay as an anchorage during easterly gales was again highlighted during a storm in 1745. The *Royal George*, an East Indiaman, collided with the *Cape Coast* (bound for Africa) which sank and was lost; the *Expedition* (on passage to Lisbon) was driven ashore at Berry Head; the *Tiger* (taking troops to Newfoundland) was also wrecked at Berry Head with the loss of 180 lives; and others were damaged in minor collisions.

There were, however, still many years of action afloat before the Battle of Trafalgar finally confirmed the supremacy of the British Navy above all others. Quiberon Bay on the west coast of France was one of the stepping-stones to this supremacy. The main part of the French Fleet was based in the narrow harbour of Brest and a close blockade was set up with the aim of preventing either the reinforcing of the armies of Montcalm in Canada or from joining with a Russo-Swedish fleet intending to mount an invasion from Ostend.[5] The most convenient place from which to mount this blockade was of course Torbay, as westerly gales spelt danger to both sides; ships could so easily be dashed up on the rocky shore near Cape Ushant.

Fortunately the bad weather which drove the British hastily north kept the Frenchmen in harbour as well. After a war of attrition had been waged for some months the French Admiral Conflans was ordered to sea, although it was known that Edward Hawke, who had taken command of the Channel Fleet, was on constant watch for any such move by him. In November yet another storm forced the latter back into Torbay for just three days. This gave Conflans the opportunity he needed to slip out southwards to pick up his transports, which were also being blockaded near the mouth of the Loire. Hawke, his flag newly hoisted on the *Royal George*, met up with him at Quiberon and a great victory for the British resulted in spite of the sickness which was prevalent in their ships; this was typhus, the scourge much feared by all seamen.[6] As a result of the Treaty of Paris which ended this particular conflict, control of both India and Canada passed into Britain's hands. She was mistress of the seas as well.

Peace lasted for just 13 years before the American colonies declared their independence in 1776 and ships were again being fitted out to reduce the likelihood of loss. Almost immediately a completely new adversary was sighted off south Devon: a large New England-built sloop with carriage-guns and at least 40 armed men on board was spotted by local pilots near the Start and off Berry Head shortly after. The first American privateer had arrived. Eighteen months later two captured prizes, laden with rice and indigo, were brought into Torquay by one of HM frigates.

France joined in the quarrel, and almost immediately both naval and merchant vessels were at anchor again, sometimes in very great numbers. In May 1778 a large convoy was heading west in the Channel bound for America and the West Indies under the guard of a squadron commanded by Admiral Arbuthnot, when a signal was received that Jersey was in danger of occupation. The whole fleet of 344 merchant-men, some armed, were dispatched into the Bay forthwith where they lay for three weeks with their tops'ls loose, awaiting the return of the Navy. Demand for food and water must have been immense. The local Turnpike Trust had been formed some years earlier and for the first time provisions could be brought in from a wide area of south Devon along the improving road network.

Spain declared war in June and at once a French fleet left Brest to join them. An army of 40,000 men was made ready to cross the Channel as soon as supremacy at sea had been gained. The following spring a large combined French and Spanish fleet was observed off Plymouth, and there was great alarm throughout the county that an invasion was imminent. The Fleet under Sir Charles Hardy sought sanctuary in Torbay but the lack of land defences was so obvious that a company of the Devon Militia was sent to Brixham to help land stores and munitions. There was no invasion and the fears subsided. During the remaining years of this war, Torbay was used mainly as the point of departure for convoys to the Americas, Newfoundland and Ireland. Admirals with famous names were there also; among them Kempenfelt, Howe and Rodney, the last sailing out to take command of the West Indies Fleet.

With the more enlightened treatment of criminals in the twentieth century it is often forgotten that one of the harsh penalties meted out to wrongdoers 200 years ago was transportation, perhaps for life, to the colonies. On 13th March 1784 the captain of HMS *Helena* then anchored in Torbay sent a message to the Governor of Exeter Prison: "Sir, a ship arrived here last night with convicts who rose about 10 days since of the master and crew. Sixty landed the same night at Paignton and escaped. The master informs me that they are a desperate set of fellows and may commit many depredations .... Signed George Cadman, Capt."[7] This transport, with nearly 200 convicts on board, was outward bound from London for Baltimore when the prisoners took over. The number who landed may have been as high as 116; 40 more who were making a similar attempt the next day were re-captured after a hand-to-hand fight before they could reach the shore. Several of the original group were also recaptured later. Altogether 24 were tried at a special Assize held in Exeter before Mr Justice Heath. They were all sentenced to death but this was subsequently "respited"; presumably they were transported for life instead.

Although the Revolution in France commenced in 1789 it was not until 1793, after the execution of Louis XVI, that war was declared. The period of relative calm, during which the Grand Fleet had been seen in the Bay only once or twice, was over and the Navy was back in force.[8] The small but growing watering-place of Torquay was encouraged to develop quickly as officers sought accommodation for their wives and families. This time the Government realised that Torbay must be properly defended, and promptly bought up land at Furzeham and on Berry Head.[9] The forts were not, however, built until some years later. The convoys were at anchor again; one for the Mediterranean left with over 700 ships in it: possibly the biggest concentration ever seen at one time - though according to eye-witnesses, the pre-D-Day operations were of great magnitude.

Possibly with the view of guarding against a recurrence of the Channel Fleet's mutiny the previous year but also to counter a possible invasion, an Order in Council created the Sea Fencibles in 1798. Recruitment was limited to fishermen, boatmen and others exempt from impressment. Members were volunteers but were under the command of naval officers and they were paid a shilling a day when on service. Torbay was included in the district which stretched from the Teign to Rame Head. There were 11 officers and 378 men and it was a force to be reckoned with. The Brixham contingent was called out during the *Venerable* affair but they do not seem to have been needed elsewhere.

Natural hazards took their toll in times of both war and peace. During this period the brig *Biscay* went ashore on Torre Abbey sands and was a total loss. Her valuable cargo went into the homes of the local wreckers.[10] Later HMS *Cambrian* was struck by lightning and three men killed, others "much scorched".

Newspapers first appeared in Exeter and Sherborne in the middle of the eighteenth century so it can be said that Devon's role during the Napoleonic Wars was the first to be covered by the Press. Certainly details of many happenings were recorded; for example, when Earl St Vincent's fleet was anchored in May 1800, one member of a boat's crew lost a pound note over the side. Immediately six jumped overboard to recover it and would have drowned, "had not two privates of Captain Eastley's Volunteer Company, then exercising on the beach, stripped off and swam to their assitance." The report concludes: "Five were rescued, one drowned."

Nelson at Torre Abbey

In October 1800 the Earl was forced to leave his flagship *Ville de Paris* because he was in poor health and had a violent cough. With the permission of the Admiralty the Commander-in-Chief took a house in

Torquay but he seems to have spent much time with his relative Mr Cary at Torre Abbey. While there he was visited on two occasions by Horatio Nelson, the newly appointed Vice-Admiral of the Blue who was then in dispute with his superior over prize money he considered due to him. There seems to have been no acrimony, as he confided in a letter to Lady Hamilton: " .... the Earl received me with much apparent cordiality and we parted this morning good friends; but not a word about the prize money which I will certainly not give up." The invalid must have recovered sufficiently by the end of January, when he attended an elegant ball and supper given by Mr Cary to celebrate his birthday. It was the occasion for "several grand entertainments" which were graced "by all the beauty and fashion of the neighbourhood, as also by the nobility and gentry." The festivities lasted a week: there was a masquerade and "refreshments which were served up with elegance and hospitality." By February 1801 St Vincent had recovered, and was able to leave Torquay for London to take the office of First Lord of the Admiralty. For the record, Nelson benefited too: after a long drawn out legal action he received all the money due.

Early in 1803 a Royal Proclamation was read throughout the land announcing a general thanksgiving "for the end of the late bloody, extended and extensive wars in which we have been engaged." Only a few months later a "fleet of observation" was assembling in the Bay "in view of the probable renewal of war with France." With that renewal the fear of invasion returned. A crowded public meeting was held at the Crown and Anchor Inn where "a respectable and numerous gathering" unanimously approved plans for the evacuation of the town, "except for the infirm and children under the age of 8 years, who are incapable of walking ten miles in one day." The threat of invasion returned again in 1940 after the fall of France; this time however emphasis was on the *defence* of the beaches and other landing places rather than on a general retreat into the countryside.

November 1804 saw the notorious wreck of the *Venerable*. It brought the worst local crowd behaviour ever known when the folk of Paignton and surrounding villages flocked to the wreck and pillaged it. A month later HMS *Blond* went ashore in a gale. The Torbay fishermen, unable to launch their boats from Brixham, hauled them on carts a distance of four miles before succeeding from the beach nearest the wreck. Perhaps they felt they were making amends for the others.

The day of the last great sea-fight for more than a century was approaching. On 21st October 1805 the fleets of Britain, Spain and France met off Cape Trafalgar in what was to become the most famous battle of them all.

Throughout the remainder of the Napoleonic period the Channel Fleet continued to use Torbay from time to time, but the emphasis quickly changed from ships-of-war to ships-of-pleasure. On 18th September 1812 it was reported that "the day was fine and the bay was crowded with gentlemen's yachts and boats of every description." It was the day of the annual races and in the evening there was a ball at Poulton's Hotel in Torquay "attended by all the beauty and fashion in that delightful watering place."

The Bellerophon at Anchor

The final act in this particular drama and the third great event in Torbay's maritime history began on Monday 24th July 1815 when the British man-of-war *Bellerophon* and her escort the corvette *Myrmidon* anchored near to Orestone at the north end. She had orders from the Admiralty to "stand out three leagues to sea and await orders." Captain Maitland, her master, had instructions that he should "prohibit all communication with the shore", but the sea was soon thronged with small boats of all sizes from as far away as Sidmouth. The crowds had poured out to see the ex-Emperor Napoleon I, prisoner of the British, who was on board. The circumstances which led to the disclosure of this star captive's presence were described by one of the seamen aboard who wrote to Chatham:

> My dear wif it would done you good to se so Many Boats around our Ship the Custom house boat Came to Inquire where our Ship was from we could not let them along side during the time that we were calling to them to let them know that no boat was to Come near our Ship the french Generall Came upon Deck and they saw him they pulled a shore and Gave it out that Bonuparte was on board our ship in tow howers there was nearly 200 Boats around our Ship men women and children gaping and looking wanting to se Bonuparte.[11]

As the news spread along the coast, more and more craft came into the Bay until it resembled a regatta day. There were so many small boats about that confusion reigned; it has been estimated that a thousand trips a day were being made: everyone wanted to see Napoleon. Captain Maitland ordered the boats to be lowered and the crew to row guard around it to keep the eager lookers-on at a distance. Many however did get near enough to have a good view of the prisoner, and an eye-witness report appeared in the *News*, "a weekly newspaper: being a faithful and comprehensive digest .... published in London at an early hour on Sunday" under the dateline: Dartmouth July 26:

> Bonaparte walks on deck till six o'clock. He shows himself to spectators round the ship, on retiring he pulls off his hat. He appears often to be looking at people through his eye-glass and his picture which appeared in London, is an exact likeness of him. He wears a dark green coat, with red collar buttoned close; cocked hat .... light tan knee breeches and stockings of the same colour. Every person on the quarter-deck, both French and English, remain with their heads uncovered when he is on deck.

A serving British naval officer saw him rather differently.[12] In a letter to his brother, T.Bond wrote:

> Did you see that scoundrel and murderer Napoleon when in Torbay. If you make a journey here and you will meet with no difficulty if the weather should be fine as he regularly shows himself .... His face is broad, flat and of a swarthy colour with a black stiff beard. I think that his highth must by 5ft.6 inches or under ....

Even a defeated enemy was treated as a gentleman; Napoleon had aboard with him his aide-de-camp, a Counsellor of State and other officers, his surgeon and about 40 servants. Mr Cary of Torre Abbey sent out presents of fresh fruit from his kitchen garden to the "hero of modern Europe", as one contemporary historian described him. British sailors on the other hand viewed their important prisoner with less respect; the *News* explained: "Our jolly tars, with their usual good humour, put out a board chalked 'He's gone to dine!'"

On Wednesday 2nd August the *Bellerophon* and the *Tonnant* sailed off to Plymouth where it was proposed that Napoleon be transferred to the *Northumberland*. There were similar scenes in Plymouth as thousands flocked to see him. It was however discovered that a writ of *habeas corpus* was being sought in the High Court, so the two ships were hurriedly recalled to Torbay, sailing from the Sound only minutes before the subpoena arrived. Off Berry Head the *Northumberland*, sailing west from Portsmouth, encountered them coming towards her and all three anchored inside the Bay. Immediately this had been completed Sir Henry Bunbury went on board the *Bellerophon* and told Napoleon of the British Cabinet's decision, which was that he should be transported to St Helena with four of his friends, chosen by himself, and 12 domestics. He expressed no surprise at this as he had been reading the English newspapers and was well aware of the speculation in them, but he did protest against it in a cool, well reasoned speech which lasted three-quarters of an hour. Later Lord Keith, Admiral of the Channel Fleet, informed him personally that he would be transferred immediately to HMS *Northumberland* for the journey to his island prison. Napoleon replied that he refused to go, whereupon Lord Keith reminded him that it was the decision of the Government and he would be forced into the "necessity of resorting to coercive measures." Bonaparte's response according to one account[13] was "Oh,no,no,no. You command, I must obey …. but I do not go of my own free will."

The transfer of all baggage began early in the morning of Monday 7th August. It included his plate, several articles of gold and 4,000 gold napoleons which were all the ex-Emperor had brought with him when he left France.

The final act of the drama was conducted with pomp and ceremony. Promptly at 11.30 am Lord Keith, using Tonnant's barge, went aboard *Bellerophon* and received Napoleon and the distinguished individuals who, with their families, had "resolved to share his fate". The whole party then descended the gangway to the barge, Napoleon pausing before he stepped off the bottom step to "doff his hat" as a farewell gesture to his first captors. On the deck of the *Northumberland* the Captain's guard of marines had assembled on the poop with their arms and with a drum ready to beat a roll thrice, the usual salute to a general

Napoleon on deck of the Bellerophon *(W. Orchardson painting in the National Maritime Museum. Reproduced with kind permission)*

Napoleon in Torbay; sight-seers embarking, 1815 (TNHS)

The Bellerophon *in Torbay, July 1815*

officer in the British service. Behind them the quarter-deck was crowded with officers, including some of senior rank who had found it opportune to be posted to Torbay for the occasion. As the barge crossed the narrow stretch of water between the two battle-ships there was a total silence in the official party and a respectful quiet among the many spectators. As Napoleon slowly mounted the gangway the guard presented arms, the drums rolled and after making the brief statement: "Je suis à vos ordres", he went below.

Interest however remained intense, the *Northumberland* now being the object of the seaborne sightseers' interest. The very same day there occurred an unfortunate accident with loss of life:

.... A boat from Torquay, having on board three ladies, one gentleman, one child, one servant and two boatmen went out to witness the transfer .... to the *Northumberland*. As she was sailing around the head of the latter vessel, she was met by a King's cutter and before each was aware of the approach of the other, the boat was run down and instantly sunk. The Lieutenant of the *Northumberland* witnessing the distressing scene, leapt into the sea and succeeded in saving one of the ladies (Mrs Harris) and the child from a watery grave. [The rest were also saved except for] two ladies (both young), an aunt and a niece, sunk to rise no more.[14]

Only three days after this sad affair the small fleet carrying "the scourge of Europe" was outward-bound and the most profitable time ever for the local boatmen had ended.

VI SEAMEN ASHORE AND AFLOAT

The Press Gang

Press-ganging men is one of the oldest and worst features of British naval history and dates back several centuries. In 1627, for example, the Earl of Denbigh then at Plymouth was granted a warrant valid in all three south-west counties "for the leavying and impresting of marriners." About 20 years later continuing wars meant that the finding of sufficient crew was becoming increasingly difficult. When hostilities began against the Dutch, it was said that at first men flocked to join the Navy's vessels but as in many wars the numbers required were greater than the number of volunteers, so the only answer was impressment. There were also counter-attractions. Privateering offered better financial rewards and the developing Newfoundland trade tempted away men who would normally have been willing to serve. As has already been seen, the pirate John Nutt obtained his crews by offering good, regular pay which was something the Navy of the day could not do.

The press-master was often himself a retired naval captain and he was issued with a warrant authorising him to obtain men for the Fleet. Payment was based on numbers obtained and the method used was for the "Gang" to seize their victim and force him to accept a shilling. The taking of the King's money was deemed to form a contract and he could be carried aboard a man-of-war; in this area he would have been taken straight on to a ship anchored in Torbay.

In the seventeenth century the Vice-Admiral of Devon was in charge of the impressment service but the actual work was done by the local mayors; in 1664 Thomas Newman submitted a list of men and an account of the charges incurred by him as Mayor of Dartmouth.[1] There were problems finding the numbers needed; it was explained that only 200 men had been "pressed" in the whole of Devon, possibly because the "remissness of the (local) constables not a little prejudices the business, instead of executing the warrants, they give the seamen notice to escape."

A hundred years later, during the War of American Independence, the Navy was itself in charge, as local events confirm. Eighteenth century Devon had a regular newspaper, the *Flying Post*, and in 1778 it was reported that Rowland Phillips, a midshipman on HMS *Princess Royal*, was on trial in Exeter charged with the murder of a man called Collier, master of a Torquay fishing-smack. In June he was brought before the King's Bench for judgment. While he was pressing men for the Navy he fired several shots to bring the vessel to halt. One of these shots hit Collier and killed him. Phillips was found not guilty of murder but of the lesser charge of manslaughter because he was acting in the execution of his duties and "without personal resentment." His sentence was "burning in the hand" which was carried out immediately. This punishment dated back to the sixteenth century and was a form of branding.

The Navy was still desperate for men. So many were being "pressed" from Dartmouth and its neighbourhood that the Newfoundland trade was "in a distressed state, from the loss of the great number of fishermen and seamen already impressed .... and the impossibility of procuring others to work on board the vessels fitting out, from the strictness of the officers employed in the impress service."[2]

As soon as the Napoleonic War broke out the great need of men arose again, so the Press Gang, which had never ceased operating, had to be re-introduced when other means failed. Bounties were offered in inland places for those who volunteered, but their numbers were far below those required, so in March 1795 an Act was passed which required men to be raised by every county in England and Wales.[3] Shortly after, the protection of fishermen from impressment was stopped and the ports were required to contribute men as well. Other concessions were made, but still the right kind of men were not forthcoming, so in 1801 a Royal Pardon was offered to deserters who surrendered themselves. This reliance by the Navy on "pressed men" greatly concerned its

Physician Dr Trotter, whose work is told in more detail later. He considered the 1795 Act which recruited "requisitioned seamen and landsmen" a precedent which might be "initiated in any future emergency: a country which boasts of her civil rights should long ago have been rescued from involuntary engagement."[4] This was very progressive thinking two centuries ago. He went on to say that "the evils of impressment are manifold; a great number of our best seamen disappear at the beginning of a war and conceal themselves." As a result it took time to crew vessels. The men were crowded together, they had to sleep on deck and some, particularly those from country areas, were not clean, "without cloathes", and so spread infection. The crews of many newly-commissioned ships were so sickly that they could not be considered an effective force for some time after the commencement of hostilities.

The Fleet in Torbay continued to need the Press Gang to supplement its numbers for several years more. When an advertisement appeared in the *Flying Post* in 1803 for stonemasons to build a new pier at Torquay (the present inner harbour) there was a footnote promising that "persons undertaking this work will be guaranteed protection against the activities of the Press Gang" - a very necessary aid to recruitment, as the men would have come in from a wide area of south Devon. This was just at the time that an Admiral on a ship anchored in Torbay was issuing an order that:

Each Captain should select from the crew of the HM ship under your command a sufficient number of trusty and well-disposed men to man three boats, with as many marines and petty officers as you may judge necessary to send in each, under the orders of a lieutenant, to whom you will deliver a press warrant .... And you are likewise to select 16 marines that may be trusted, to stop up the avenues leading up to the country .... You will endeavour to have previous communication with one of His Majesty's Justices of the Peace, applying to him to back the warrants, taking especial care to cause as little alarm as possible .... On the boats returning to the ships, you will make a return to me of the number and quality of the men that you may have impressed.[5]

. It was not only the innocent young men of the district who were "shanghaied" to sea in one manner or another. Wrongdoers, including local smugglers and wreckers, were "put aboard men-of-war" - Jack Rattenbury, the notorious east Devon smuggler was one. Once a man was on the ship he stayed there; this was the usual practice during the Napoleonic War. Shore leave was rarely if ever granted and then only for the most compassionate reasons. Living conditions were arduous; there was little light, it was frequently wet below as the timbers leaked (during one influenza-type outbreak the decks of the *Colossus* were cleaned with sand instead of water on the orders of the surgeon). Fresh water was scarce and the discipline was harsh and callous.[6] In spite of all these privations Dr Trotter, who was himself in the Bay from time to time, had a high regard for his ordinary seamen; he said of them:

> A true-bred seaman is rarely a profligate character .... hence he plays the rogue with awkward grace though with a degree of cunning. In his pleasures he is coarse, and in his person slovenly: he acquires no experience from past misfortunes and is heedless of futurity .... But his virtues are of the finest cast. In the hour of battle he has never left his officer to fight alone .... in his friendships he is warm, sincere and untinctured by selfish views .... His real diseases spring from the causes peculiar to a sea life: laborious duty, change of climate, and inclement seasons, bring on premature age and few of them live to be old.[7]

It was when seamen deserted that the most grim punishments were meted out. Keel-hauling and "flogging through the fleet" were the most notorious. The former involved the recipient being attached to the middle of a rope which was passed under the keel and the sentence was carried out by passing the bound man underneath a specific number of times resulting in half drowning and having much of his skin rubbed off by barnacles. No instances of this happening in Torbay are known but following the court martial of Peter White in 1748 on HMS *Victory* for desertion, his punishment was "twenty lashes on his bare back alongside each of the flagships, and 40 alongside the *Torbay*, the ship to which he belonged," one hundred strokes of the "cat-o'-nine-tails" in all. This was done with full naval ceremony and before the crews of all the ships who had been specially mustered for the occasion.

Press Gangs went soon after the War, in 1815, but the "cat" took a long time to disappear. The Admiralty tried to abolish it and from 1852 quarterly returns were required to be submitted to Parliament. In 1871 its use was suspended, and from 1879 for all practical purposes it was abolished.[8] The final formal step to do so has however never been taken. Flogging was always a frequently awarded punishment. As late as the 1830s there were still many severe and often brutal captains in the Service, to whom the verdicts of flogging and other eccentric punishments were outlets for their sadistic natures.

Hanging from the yard-arm was the ultimate penalty for the most serious crimes of murder and mutiny. This sentence was implicit when William Lee and Thomas Preston were court-martialled in 1797 on board the Royal *Sovereign* at anchor in Torbay for "endeavouring to stir up mutiny in the crew" and of attempting to murder John Graham, boatswain's mate. They were sentenced and executed on the 4th September.

Caring for the Sick and Hurt
While the problem of sick sailors was an ongoing one, the large fleets which assembled during the sixteenth and seventeenth centuries presented a serious consequence to the local inhabitants - the men were unceremoniously cast ashore and left to fend for themselves. Unusually however the earliest items in a Paignton churchwarden's account book relate to people who came into Torbay from overland. After the Cadiz expedition in 1625 soldiers billeted in Dartmouth brought disease with them, and there were other strangers to be helped as well:

    1628 Paid for convaying away the souldiers ....
    1629 Paid four Englishmen taken by Dunkirkers ....
    1630 Paid to a ffrenchman ....
    1630 Paid to one John Bowden of Dartmouth taken by the
          Spaynyards ....

All were given amounts of money. Clearly therefore the local parishioners were offering relief to outsiders; so too were inland villages like Chudleigh, where a highway from a port passed through it.[9] A few years later, in 1637, when John Spurway was mayor of Dartmouth, he complained that "great numbers of French prisoners in a destitute condition have been landed in Torbay by Dunkirk men-of-war."[10] This time, however, the overseers must have been less willing to help, as no entries have been found in the year's disbursements. The needs of the Paignton poor were taking all the available money. The activities of the Press Gang must have inflamed tempers too; having their prime youth taken from them by force and left with the sick and inept rejects was no doubt more than they could tolerate. Sometimes money arrived from the Government, probably only when the numbers involved were small. In 1692 £9.12s. was disbursed by the Treasury "for the use of several houses in Brixom to lodge sick men in." Later, in 1696, their Lordships were confronted with a demand for money as there were "from the Grand Fleet above 700 sick seamen at Torbay and the people not able to provide for them."[11] Soon the situation must have have deteriorated even further because in April 1697 there was a petition from Torbay saying that there were now "1500 men put ashore, the petitioners commiserating them, took them into their homes and took care of them, which reduced them to great poverty." In July the Commons asked to be enabled "to provide for the sick seamen set ashore", but it was clear that the long wars had exhausted the Treasury and that nothing could be done. Two years later yet another petition was sent from the "innholders, victuallers, and others, poor inhabitants of Dartmouth, Kingswere, Brixham and other parts of Torbay, who pray that their debt of £1500 upwards for entertaining sick and wounded seamen might be paid." The reply sent back was ambiguous: "My Lords will make provision for this and other debts relative to the sick and wounded seamen as soon as they are enabled."

As has already been seen, large numbers of ships were in Torbay over the next hundred years. Consequently during that century burial parties were landed from ships and graves dug at any convenient spot. When foundations were being laid for houses during Victorian times, human remains were often uncovered. Finds are known to have been made at Meadfoot, near Torre Abbey, and elsewhere. Bodies of drowned people found on beaches were dealt with quite differently;

some were buried where they were found, others were taken to a local churchyard to be given a formal burial. Church Rate account books for Paignton parish show that a regular procedure was followed. Men watched by the body while a messenger was dispatched on horseback to Totnes for the coroner. It was then buried in the churchyard, the parish paying for transport, coffin and grave-diggers. The latter were always given beer in addition to a cash payment for the arduous work.

By the end of the eighteenth century the health of seamen was gaining some attention and the man who did much to improve their conditions was Thomas Trotter, MD, Physician to His Majesty's Fleet during the Napoleonic War period. His researches went into great depth and were eventually published in three volumes in 1804.[12] There are frequent references to the fleet in Torbay and particularly to the events which led to the setting up of a naval hospital at Goodrington.

During the 1790s it was policy to equip one vessel as a hospital ship and station it with the Channel Fleet in Torbay. One of these was the *Medusa* (50 guns) which was fitted out at Plymouth late in 1796. Men sick of the scurvy were treated on board their own ships, but the more serious cases (ulcers and pulmonic complaints are quoted) were transferred to the *Medusa* from which they were later discharged either to Haslar (Portsmouth) or to Plymouth. However in 1799 "the sick of the Fleet suffered severely from having no hospital ship in Torbay during the winter months. Those that were sent ashore in Torbay were frequently carried to Dartmouth, five miles distance, in open carts, there being no hospital in Brixham." This is amplified in a diary-type entry for August the following year:

In consequence of very just complaints made by the surgeon of the *Ville de Paris* to Earl St Vincent at Torbay in May last, his Lordship was pleased to make representations to the Admiralty on the necessity of fitting some hospital for the accommodation of the sick. At the Sick Quarters of Dartmouth, men in fevers were lying two and two in a bed! While an hospital ship was attached to the Fleet, there seemed no want of a Sick Quarters in Torbay, but the former Commander in Chief, having suggested the dismission of that ship, it is rather unkind to perceive the Channel Fleet so ill provided, as appears from this complaint. A Commissioner of Sick and Hurt was therefore ordered to Torbay to inspect those ghastly retreats of sickness; and a large dwelling house near the beach was directed to be fitted up immediately for the reception of our people.

Matters did not move fast enough for Dr Trotter; two months later he recorded "there was even a necessity of sending joiners and carpenters from the ships to accelerate the building - when I look around and see the splended edifices rising everywhere for the use of the army, my heart bleeds for the neglected navy."

During part of 1800 the Channel Fleet were off Ushant for a total of 121 days.[13] It was predicted that there would be many sick seamen among the 15,000 on board the various ships; in fact only 16 had to be landed. Whether these were accommodated at "Peignton" is not certain as the date of arrival of the first batch of patients is not known. An undated entry in the *Medicina* reports that the *Majestic* was no sooner at sea than a typhus appeared and spread with great speed through the crew, 13 of whom died. Many more stayed on the sick list and the Commander-in-Chief "thought it proper to order her to Torbay where she landed fifty people at Mr Ball's Hospital." Mr Ball's Hospital was the name given to the Goodrington establishment, Dr Ball being the surgeon-in-charge. About the same time, probably in November, the *Donegal* landed 28 men suffering from typhus after some had died on board because the weather had been too bad for them to be landed earlier. On 20th December the *Pompee*'s surgeon, Mr Lind, diagnosed smallpox in a man who had been ashore in Plymouth but which had not manifested itself until after arrival in Torbay. He was taken ashore to the hospital.

Being on the staff at Goodrington was a hazardous occupation. One of the patients from the *Majestic* infected Mr Ball and others and all had the disease to a severe degree. Six people died and Mr Stevenson, another surgeon, had to be transferred from Haslar to take over the former's duties for some time. Whether or not Mr Ball recovered sufficiently to resume is not stated but he was certainly not there in 1808 because in June Mr Willes the surgeon died at the early age of 39, probably from one of the dread diseases, and was interred in Paignton churchyard. During the 1790s men - and women - who had died on HM ships were carried ashore and buried there as the Parish burials record shows. Some time after the hospital was established a burial ground came into use on the north side. It is generally agreed that this was consecrated by the Bishop George Pelham on 28th September 1808. A considerable number of officers and men were interred there and some had stones put up to their memory. By the middle of the nineteenth century it was in a sad state of neglect and the ground was being rapidly washed away by the sea.[14] Although the hospital had been sold to a Colonel Drake of Ipplepen in 1822, the Admiralty must have retained an interest in the burial ground because it authorised the restoration of the sea defences by two local contractors. Today the only memorial stone which survives is one to Major Thomas Hill of the 47th Regiment of Foot who died in the hospital on 22nd July 1815. There were still several simple graves to be seen at Goodrington early this century but the development of the pleasure area over the past 60 years there has caused the destruction of all other evidence of the old burial ground.

The medical establishment of Dr Trotter's day did not readily accept the existence of the new Paignton hospital; sick sailors continued to be transferred by sea just as they always have been! The Doctor wrote disapprovingly:

> Instead of the hospital at Torbay being a place of rest for the sick and hurt of the fleet, it appears, a system of service, as conducted here, has added much to their affliction. After remaining on shore for a few days, they are sometimes sent round to Haslar or to Plymouth hospital in unfavourable weather.

In those early days the surgeon too was considered of more junior status and it was not until 1809 that his salary was increased to £500 a year, a considerable sum for those days. In addition there was a barracks and men stationed there undertook guard duties at Goodrington and on Berry Head. The hospital closed in 1816, just about a year after the end of hostilities.

A Place for Water and Victuals

From the sixteenth century onwards vast numbers of ships anchored in Torbay. Many required stores but they needed water even more. The little village of Torquay had a fair-sized stream known as the Fleet, which flowed into the sea near the Haven; the pier was unlikely to have been in a sufficiently sound condition to take the weight of heavy barrels and the many seamen who would have to handle them. They therefore descended on Brixham Quay instead. There were streams running down the two valleys which fed a large mill-pool. A surviving letter dated March 1672[15] notes that HM ships had obtained their supplies "for as long as the memory of man reacheth back." It went on to outline an ambitious scheme using deal boards to make "a large square vessel …. to receive the water from the mill-pool and from thence there may be as many small conveyances made (also of deal) as will at once fill as many casks as the stream will afford to do." It is also proposed that "a bank must be taken off for the easier rolling of casks to and from the sea." The cost of the work was estimated to be "less than thirty pounds all prepared in a month's time or less …." It took rather longer than that - just over a century.

Perhaps a start was made, as Kings Quay is believed to have been built about 1690, but the improvements at Devonport may have meant that further works at Brixham were unnecessary. The Navy however preferred Torbay and in 1693 orders were given that large quantities of beer be stored at Dartmouth in readiness for its arrival in the Bay. A supply of good beer was essential for the health of the ships' companies; there were complaints from time to time about the quality. Shortly after this 24 Dutch and 45 English men-of-war were at anchor; "beer, beef, pork, biscuits, pease, oatmeal, stockfish [salted hake] , butter and cheese for 24000 men" were taken out to them by victualling ships. The seamen of William III were clearly better fed than their predecessors.

To cope with the fleets in the eighteenth century the Eastern Quay was built at Brixham about 1760, but no other major developments were undertaken until 1781, when plans were drawn up for a Naval Reservoir with an underground pipeline of wood to Deer Rock. Most accounts say that the work was completed in 1801. Dr Trotter noted rather ambiguously late the previous year:

Brixham Harbour about 1900; note sail lofts and barking sheds; Kings Quay adjacent (TL)

The watering duty is however a great draw back to the health of the fleet. Strange, that a few pounds should be put in competition with so vast an object! I would have the seamen and marines of a fleet fed and exercised in a manner which would preserve them in the highest possible strength .... But the water of Torbay, like other ports, ought to be supplied to them, for it unnecessarily exposes a number of men to severity of weather.[16]

The Naval Reservoir in Brixham town centre (lithograph about 1840)

From this it is obvious that either water was not being drawn from the reservoir then or that the Doctor was unaware it was being built. Brixham Town Hall now stands on the site of the old Reservoir.

There was also a wry comment by him (in 1803) that the Fleet "continues with a few exceptions to enjoy the most perfect health. The fatigue of severe sea-duty has been prevented during some hard gales; all scurvy is overcome by the long use of fresh meat and vegetable refreshments; and the exposure to drinking spirituous liquors in great measure done away with by keeping the men on board." One ship, the *Naiad*, acknowledged receiving "beef and turnips by the order of Earl

Fleet in Torbay about 1912; view from the Royal Terrace Gardens in Torbay Road

St Vincent which has been of great use in recruiting the strength of our people."

The build-up of the Royal Navy shortly before the outbreak of the 1914-18 War brought large numbers of ships and men into the Bay again. In 1912 there was a mock battle off South Devon where the "X" and "Y" forces were deployed. The task of feeding the sailors was the responsibility of local tradesmen including:

> Messrs Slades .... and Mr R.Blatchford and the prices of commodities - butter, cream, etc., advanced in consequence of the huge demand. In readiness for the Fleet there had been conveyed to the stores on Beacon Quay, scores of carcases of cattle and sheep and hundreds of sacks of potatoes .... [17]

Originally between 130 and 140 ships were expected with crews totalling 60,000 men. Rather less than these numbers actually arrived. Torquay had long since had a sweet water supply from Dartmoor and it was with this that the Fleet tenders were filled for transfer in huge quantities to the anchored warships. Torbay water is still much sought after by all vessels both large and small.

Signal Stations around Torbay

Only a short time ago Brixham coastguards were required to be "good lamp-men" because Aldis lamps were used daily to communicate with small coasters and other vessels approaching the Bay or on passage to the east. These have now been superseded by VHF (very high frequency) radio networks. In much the same way signal lamps replaced the slow and cumbersome semaphore. When the Coastguard was part of the Royal Navy, routine communication was carried out with "flags", but at Brixham the men were required to operate a tall semaphore with metal arms which stood at the extreme end of Berry Head. Geoffrey Wilson[18] has made a detailed study of how various methods of sending messages between ship and shore were tried out and later abandoned for an "improved system."

The earliest seen in Devon was the fire beacon. As already noted, these burned fiercely to warn of the imminent arrival of the Spanish

Armada. By the time war was declared against Napoleon's France the need was realised for a standard method of relaying signals between HM ships and the shore, so in 1794 a start was made on a number of land stations all the way along the south coast. Standard codes using flags, pendants and black balls were adopted, and these were raised on old ships' top-masts which had been fixed in position on exposed headlands. The one at Brixham was set up in 1795 and was under the charge of a naval lieutenant, a midshipman and two seamen.[19] Another was put up at Coleton (Down End) above Dartmouth.[20] Messages were passed only between ships in or approaching Torbay, and no attempt was made to communicate with neighbouring shore stations. The need to pass urgent messages was appreciated, so between 1795 and 1796 a shutter telegraph chain was established by the Admiralty between London and Deal. This was later extended to Portsmouth and finally to Plymouth.[21] Torbay was bypassed, the nearest stations being at Chudleigh and at Great Haldon (hence "Telegraph Hill").[22] Telescopes were fixed in such a way that they could only read the shutters on either side, and the movement of ships locally could not be passed directly to London. It was reported that complete messages could however be passed between the capital and Plymouth in 15 minutes. This line closed down in 1814 when the telescopes were returned to the Admiralty and the men paid off. About the same time orders were given for the south coastal stations to be "broken up".

Across the Channel in France the semaphore had been invented and in 1812 a British system which was a direct copy was operating on the east coast. Before long the semaphore was the only accepted method and one invented by Sir Home Popham was adopted for a new telegraph from London to Portsmouth (later also approved for extension to Plymouth). It proved expensive to construct and was only put into commission as far as the Hants/Dorset border. Land was however bought or leased for the remaining stations; those of particular interest locally were named as at "Roccombe" and "Beacon Hill". The former is Great Hill at Rocombe (there is now a reservoir on top) which appears with the name "Telegraph Hill" on the nineteenth century estate-map. In 1849 the Admiralty had no further use for it so Isambard Kingdom Brunel, then the incoming "squire" at Watcombe, was unsuccessfully in the market for it. (The Crown eventually sold the land to a later owner of the estate). Beacon Hill (198 metres) behind Paignton is visible over a wide area including Berry Head. It is still used for communications purposes by the Police and as a site for the transmission of both BBC and ITV television.

Berry Head Lighthouse; the Coastguards were then part of the Admiralty and wore sailors' uniforms

The invention of the electric telegraph in mid-century made possible efficient, speedy, long-distance communication regardless of weather conditions. However, semaphore signalling remained in use in the Navy for many years: the 1910-21 edition of the Torbay Directory notes that the "Royal Naval Reserve Coastguard Station" was the Lloyds Signal Station for Torbay. Photographs show that the semaphore pole was on Berry Head before 1875 and was then probably used in conjunction with the electric telegraph office which was established in Lower Brixham in 1869. When it was taken down is not certain. The lighthouse on Berry Head, which is administered by Trinity House, was built in 1906. Nearly 70 metres above the sea its light is visible for 40 miles.

Some terms - "chain" for example - retained their connotation right up to World War II. The word was adopted by the Royal Air Force for its coastal radar stations and it is perhaps not by coincidence that a CHL (Chain, Home, Low) was commissioned near Down End (between Brixham and Kingswear) to warn Torbay and other South Devon towns of the imminent arrival of low-flying enemy aircraft. From 1942 RAF Kingswear was also undertaking standby surface-watching but later more sophisticated equipment was installed and its sea-surveillance role extended.

Paignton Coastguard Station and Harbour (about 1890)

Torquay Harbour in 1832; the "Chinese coolie hat" is a hand-crane (TL)

A working harbour: Torquay in the late 1860s

VII PEACE AND PROGRESS, 1815–1900

Arrival of the First Visitors

In 1759 Dr Richard Russel had published his treatise on the value of sea-water in the treatment of the glands. Thus began the search for healthy watering places. The improvements in the road network which followed the creation of the Turnpike Trusts in the late eighteenth century brought wealthy invalids to Sidmouth, Exmouth, Dawlish and Teignmouth, probably in that order, "to take the waters"; hence the term "watering place" rather than "the seaside". Torquay, at that time very much smaller than any of these, seems to have been discovered about 1790, when the traveller Maton was inspired to write: "Instead of the uncomfortable village we had imagined, how great was our surprise at seeing a pretty range of neat, new buildings, fitted up for summer visitors, who may here enjoy convenient bathing, retirement, and a most romantic situation."

The Navy discovered the civilian attractions of Torquay at about the same time. Another writer notes: "It was first brought into notice by the families of naval officers, stationed in the bay during the war, who bore testimony to the salubrity of the climate and to its sheltered situation."

The defeat of the French had made the Channel safe, and the invention of steam propulsion for vessels made voyage times shorter and no longer dependent on favourable winds; thus the first steamships began calling in Torbay during the early 1820s. Before 1830 the *Brunswick*, a 100 horsepower steamer, was calling on her way from Portsmouth to Plymouth. She and her successors, which included the *City of Glasgow*, ran for almost two decades right up to the arrival of the railway in 1848. A drawing of the *Brunswick* lying in Torquay harbour shows she had a funnel like a factory chimney and masts fore-and-aft with gaffs on which sails could be rigged when necessary.

The emphasis in contemporary publicity was on "invalids desirous of abridging the land journey and diversifying the route by a survey of the coast." Passengers were landed "at Torquay Pier, tide permitting." Commander Russell of the *Brunswick* naturally chose Torquay as the place for disembarking as there was both a new harbour and a road leading to it. The harbour at Paignton was in a ruinous condition until after 1838, while Brixham, although an ancient port, was still rather

QUAY~Harbour

Steamship Brunswick *in Torquay Harbour about 1840; view from Beacon Hill (TL)*

inaccessible for the carriages needed to carry off the invalids come to "seek the mildest atmosphere of ous western climate."

The early nineteenth century also saw the birth of sailing for pleasure which continues to the present day - and has led to the formation of a yacht marina in 1984. As long ago as 1830 Carrington, an early guidebook writer, proposed "such as are incapable of much bodily exertion but desire to enhale the pure sea breezes without fatigue may find a variety of pleasure yachts at hand; and no place affords greater facilities for water excursions than Torquay." The present day sailing visitor still enjoys a day's sail, however hard the effort of crewing may have been (in spite of power winches and other modern technological aids).

Seaborne Trade and Emigration The main emphasis was on commerce, as dues were needed to recoup the cost of the harbour. The growing town of Torquay, and to a lesser extent Paignton, offered great opportunities for tradesmen-entrepreneurs when totally new districts spread across the hills to the north and west of the Bay. Builders and craftsmen needed raw materials for house-building, all of which came in by sea. Culm, a low-grade coal used for lime-burning, was brought from South Wales, as were roofing slates and cement. Timber was

Torquay Harbour about 1855; Crossman vessel, possibly the Dynamene *at quay*

almost entirely imported from North America and the Baltic. General goods and provisions were brought in by Mr Slade and the others.

The new harbour was also chosen by Richard Lamble, who owned successively the *Caroline* (1810-15), the *Mayflower* (1816) and the *Brothers* (1817-27). He was engaged mainly in the London trade but the last-named vessel shared moorings with the steam-packet *Sir Francis Drake* in the Portsmouth-Plymouth trade. By 1830 "five safe vessels" were operating between Torquay and London with sailings every eight days. At the same time there were sailing vessels working out of Brixham to both Jersey and Guernsey. This was definitely the "age of the ship" though sea-trade was to suffer from the "age of the train" in later years.

The best known name in the timber trade for more than a century was Crossman of Torquay. In 1841 John Crossman was importing cargoes direct from New Brunswick in a Teignmouth brig called *Amethyst* but in 1844 he bought the full-rigged ship *Margaret* which had been built in Canada in 1826. Many vessels in the West Country trade were Canadian built and acquired by local owners through the close links which existed between Devon and the Eastern Seaboard ports of North America.

From about 1847 the *Margaret* regularly loaded cargoes there for Torquay, but there were obvious advantages in having outbound freight on the voyage back. Emigrants to Canada were the answer.[1] Posters were distributed in likely areas, handbills printed and advertisements placed in newspapers.

The number of passengers carried varied from ship to ship; for example on one voyage in 1851, 50 went to Quebec in the *Sarah Fleming*; a year later 20 went to the same destination in the *Margaret*. The Passenger Act of 1849 required a return to be made and a record book among the surviving Crossman papers lists names, ages and occupations of those carried in both the *Margaret* and *Sarah Fleming* over a period of some years. The fare from Torquay to Canada was between £3 and £3.10s. for adults and for those under fourteen £1.10s. to £2. A typical voyage time was 47 days but occasionally bad weather lengthened the transit time considerably. In 1862 the *Chronicle* reported the arrival of the *Margaret* in Dartmouth: "She was so long at sea that there were fears for her safety."

EMIGRATION TO QUEBEC, AND THE UNITED STATES.

TO SAIL, (D. V.,) on or about the 10th of APRIL, 1851, from Torquay, where she is now lying, the well-known copper fastened, and coppered BRIG,

"Sarah Fleming,"

600 Tons Burthen. THOMAS CROSSMAN, Master.

Few Vessels from the West of England are more adapted for emigrants than the "SARAH FLEMING," her decks are well fitted up and commodious, and as the owners themselves superintend the sailing of he Vessel, that no imposition of any kind can be practised on the Passengers.

Application can be obtained of the Captain on Board, or to Mr. JOHN CROSSMAN, Timber Merchant, Torquay.

Emigration from Torquay; newspaper advertisement, 1851

The brig *Sarah Fleming* was bought by the Crossmans in 1850 and Thomas was appointed master although only 22. She eventually sank in a storm in 1864 but shortly before this, while on passage from Quebec to Torquay, was found drifting water-logged and abandoned in mid-Atlantic with only a dog on board. In earlier days, if a man, dog or cat escaped alive from a derelict vessel it was technically not a wreck for salvage purposes.[2] The inference must be that the *Sarah Fleming's* animal was deliberately left on board with this in mind. The crew had been saved by another ship and there were of course no passengers carried on the west-to-east voyage.

Outward-bound emigrants must have suffered from experiences other than the weather and privations of ship-board life, as a surviving log-book of the *Margaret* shows. Before a voyage in 1851 the crew "except for the Master, Mate and 1 Ordinary" went ashore without authority. At 5 am they returned "on board in a very drunken state" but this did not delay the ship's departure. At noon the following day the master reported "crew still not clear of their drunkenness." He did however add, "the passengers all well." The Crossmans' concern for their passengers was genuine and several hundred emigrants made the voyage and settled successfully in the New World. More recently their descendants have returned to Devon in search of their "roots".

Emigrants were still leaving Torquay much later. In May 1883, 64 went to Canada in the Parisian, while in September the same year 30 left for Australia in an unnamed ship.

Across the Bay the "Paignton Harbour Company" was formed to rebuild the quays and improve the harbour. The prospectus indicated that the financial outlook for the future was good; commodities in demand were to be assessed for dues; among them was cider at 9d. a hogshead and potatoes at 1½d. a bag. In addition, 8,000 tons of shipping was expected each year (at twopence a ton) and thus the whole enterprise would be very profitable. The Act received Royal Assent in 1837 and the work was done soon after. Although the harbour was used by small brigs and schooners for the rest of the century it is doubtful if it ever produced the anticipated income. It remained in private hands until 1935, and after its transfer to the local authority the only woman harbour-master in the British Isles, Miss Gale, was appointed.

The part played by the merchant schooners of Brixham in the economy of Torbay has been largely overshadowed by the fisheries. The fleet became one of the largest on the coast and although most vessels did not work out of the town, they were largely built, owned and crewed from there. (In 1857[3] there were nearly 80 shipowners listed - a large number for a small place like Brixham). They traded in wine, fruit and general cargoes to many parts of the world and brought much additional prosperity to it.[4] In the winter months their voyages were to Portugal (for fruit) and during the summer some loaded up with iron-ore from Sharkham and other mines in the vicinity.[5] This ore they carried north, returning to Devonshire with coal. The trade had declined to virtually nothing by the turn of the century but 50 years earlier there were said to be 140 vessels (of between 60 and 185 tons) registered in Brixham.

As in previous centuries, national events continued to be mirrored in local happenings. In alliance with France the English were at war with Russia in the Crimea, so the revenue cutter Francis of Lyme was able to

From the log of the Margaret, *July 1852; the crew were drunk but the passengers, "all well". (TL)* towards *Quebec*

185 2

Remarks, &c., and Entries required by Act of Parliament.	Amount of any Fine or Forfeiture.		
	£	s.	d.
A.M. *Light winds & fine &c*			
... Topsail Tacks			
... in a bad State through			
weakness			
At 4 about the Henry Head			
... & fine &c			
At Noon All Sail Set			
... Close to the ...			
Passengers all well			

	VARIATION.	BEARINGS AND DISTANCE AT NOON.	

P.M. *Light winds & fine &c*
Hazy ... Fog at Intervals —

"New" Paignton Harbour about 1860, Torbay House (demolished 1874) in background (TL)

claim as "the first capture of the season" the Russian brigantine *Kniphause*, intercepted with false Prussian papers in May 1855. Seven years later, an American privateer sought refuge in Torbay during a January storm; whether she was Union or Confederate is not recorded. In 1859 France was again the probable enemy. Louis Napoleon's great preparations for war were causing much concern. Admiral Dacres warned that the French navy now comprised a number of first-class steam vessels which could land an army of 200,000 men during one long summer day between Sidmouth and Brixham. Steamers leaving Cherbourg at nightfall could reach any part of South Devon in seven hours. Just 12 months later Government surveyors were in the area examining the cost of fortifying the coast.

The end of that old enmity was not far away. In 1886 the French cadet ship *Bougainville* was in the Bay. Many of the crew landed to see the sights. Later on other cadet vessels were making calls which foreshadowed the forging of the *entente cordiale* 20 years later.

Perhaps the most spectacular happening of the century was the destruction of the *Wallace* by fire.[6] On 6th January 1873 the vessel, registered in the USA, was anchored, wind-bound, in the Bay when a fire was discovered in her forehold. Although only in ballast after carrying a cargo of petroleum spirit, her master decided to beach her on Paignton sands, but with rigging and sails now ablaze she was blown towards the shore and beached near the Torbay Hotel. The Princess Gardens by Torquay Harbour were not then built and the water came up to the sea-wall which formed the southern boundary of the road. The Wallace was soon a flaming fire-ball; smoke and sparks were carried into the town by rising storm winds and fire-engines had to be brought to the scene ready to extinguish minor outbreaks on shore started by the flying debris. So many people were attracted to the conflagration that all traffic was diverted. A Torquay head teacher wrote in his logbook: "A large ship on fire very close to the New Road and half the boys away to see it." By daylight the next day all that remained was the copper sheathing filled with a smouldering and smoking mass of embers.

The desire of visitors to take "trips round the bay" and to destinations along the coast has continued undiminished for nearly 200 years. The building of Haldon Pier with sheltered steps on its landward side provided the opportunity to introduce "two beautiful and powerful steam-launches *Ellie* and *Annie*." These were quite small but just 20 years later the *Duchess of Devonshire* appeared on the scene. With a capacity of 300 passengers and a speed of between 12 and 13 knots, this shallow-draught paddle-steamer was able to land her passengers directly on to South Devon's beaches down a ramp lowered on the starboard bow. (Assault craft in World War II were to adopt a similar ramp). On 13th July 1896 her sister ship the *Duke of Devonshire* made her maiden voyage and the two elegant boats were a familiar sight right up to the thirties. The *Duchess* met her end when landing passengers at Sidmouth in 1934. She swung sideways and was holed in a choppy sea.

Since the revival of the "tripper" trade after World War II, a number of operators have attempted with mixed success to bring larger vessels into service. Among the best remembered are the *Pride of Devon* and the *Princess Elizabeth*. The longest surviving is the small *Western Lady* fleet; the wooden ex-minesweepers have graced the scene for nearly 40 years and look set to continue to do so.

The paddle-steamer Duchess of Devonshire

The Duke of Devonshire *approaching Torquay*

Merchant vessels in Torquay Harbour about 1870; one of the vessels has "lost" her foremast and has a jury-rig still lashed in position

Unloading coal at Beacon Quay, Torquay in about 1880 (TL)

The Shipbuilders

An engraving by J.M.W.Turner published in January 1821 (though originally drawn some years earlier) shows the ribs of a ship, possibly a fishing-boat, under construction on stocks in a yard not far from Deer Rock at Brixham. An even earlier oil-painting shows a vessel at the same stage of building on the "beach" (now the Strand) at Torquay. These pictures are at present the only evidence that shipbuilding was being actively carried on at that time, although it is generally recognised that fishing-boats were being built at Brixham from the seventeenth century onwards.

In 1802, one of the Torquay-built craft was offered for sale in the *Flying Post*. The advertisement read: "A new vessel just launched, completely rigged with the best materials and can be sent to sea at a few days' notice." Her dimensions were given: 62 feet long, her "length aloft 70 feet" with a tonnage of "about 130 tons"; she must have been built on the beach as there is no indication of construction going on elsewhere. William Shaw had his slipway and shed under Beacon Hill

Tranquil scene in Brixham Harbour about 1910; the boy is sculling with a single oar

Brixham soon after 1800; note ship, possibly a trawler, building (Turner lithograph, first published in 1821 - TNHS)

(now the site of the Coral Island car-park) but he did not start work until later in the century. Only sparse information exists of the ships built there; in 1847 a clipper-schooner of 110 tons was launched and another very similar in 1849. Two more went down the slipway in 1850 and 1852 respectively; one of them a reasonably sized vessel of 180 tons. There is also an early photograph of a fishing-smack almost ready for launching. The last one built there was the cutter-rigged *Charlotte* in 1855. This was not long before it was engulfed in the shore-end of the new Haldon Pier.

There was also a more modest enterprise across the water on the beach under Corbyn's Head. Known grandly as Hart's Shipbuilding Establishment, it closed in 1890 after it had built, it is believed, a number of small sailing-boats. All that survives now is one faded photograph.

Brixham shipbuilders were to enjoy great prosperity for most of the nineteenth century. Early on there were at least five yards. Furneaux's was near Kings Quay with Dewdney's yard nearby, while towards Berry Head was Barter's (taken over by Jackman's who later moved next door to Upham's) and Cottie's at Shoalstone. Across the harbour at Fishcombe was a yard owned by Osborne. Other builders were Frederick Baddeley of Ranscombe (first listed in 1832), Samuel Matthews (1850) and John Richardson (1850). In mid-century, construction was under-way at Jackman's on Breakwater beach and all the paraphernalia required was stacked above high-water mark, adjacent to buildings used by his craftsmen. In times of storm this precaution was ineffective. In October 1859 "Mr Richardson, Mr Upton [ie. Upham] and Mr Dewdney lost timber to the amount of £300" and vessels under repair were washed off their stocks and badly damaged. When Holdsworth visited Brixham in 1863 he found that fishing-vessels were being built at both "Brixham and Dartmouth, a trawler costing a thousand pounds apiece." He also noted that many trawlers were being constructed at Galmpton. This yard was owned by William Gibbs in 1880. The only boat-yard operating in Torbay today is that of J.W. and A.Upham, originally founded in 1817; the Uphams at one time owned trawlers and merchant-schooners as well.

Early photograph of Shaw's Shipyard, Torquay; vessel under construction on slipway; Beacon Hill partly removed for Medical Baths

Trawler building; coal hulk in background

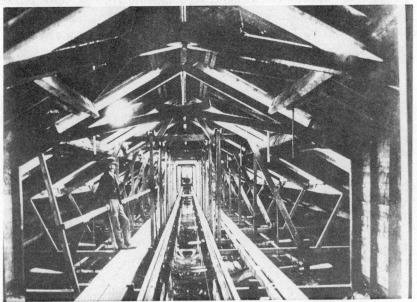

William Froude's ship-tank at Cockington, Torquay (Admiralty)

Skilled trades included shipwrights, sail and rope makers. "Patent rope-makers" included Charles Clark at Furzeham, Joseph Green also of Furzeham, and W.Green in Bolton Street; all had ceased working before 1920.

The First Ship-Tank in the World

High on the hill behind Livermead stands Chelston Cross (now the Manor House Hotel). Over a century ago a wooden shed housing a long tank filled with water stood beside it. This was the Admiralty Experiment Works set up by William Froude who moved there from Paignton in the 1860s; Having experimented with a tank in the roof of his house in Elmsleigh Road and on the River Dart, he was given £2,000 by the Government to purpose-build a long tank where he could use models to conduct experiments on the design of ships and propellers. By the time the Works moved to Haslar near Portsmouth in 1886 he had conducted 46,000 experiments. Over a century later it is still the Admiralty Experiment (not Experimental) Works - the name originally chosen by Froude for Chelston Cross. Cockington was the very first one and his pioneering work is still valued worldwide - particularly by the Japanese, who used the principles he developed to create the naval and merchant ships which have been the envy of naval architects everywhere.

VIII   THE TORBAY FISHERMEN

Catching fish for food dates back to prehistoric times. The earliest written record occurs in the foundation charter of Torre Abbey[1] when the Premonstratensian monks were granted rights to fish in the Bay. Probably fishermen started with a single hook on a line; a later development would have been to add a series of hooks on to a main warp so that larger catches could be made from one casting overboard. This led to the building of "hookers" a term which dates back to the sixteenth century or even earlier. These were quite small boats crewed by one or two men. (There were Torquay hookers working out of the harbour up to the end of the last century.)

The use of the seine, that is laying out a long net in a wide swoop around a shoal and then drawing it from both ends on to a beach, is perhaps even older. The Phoenicians may have introduced the seine into Cornwall, and some years ago members of the Devonshire Association were reminded[2] that this was the method used on the Sea of Galilee in Biblical times. Cockington fishermen used them centuries ago and bequeathed them to their children, one in 1534 "a dragnet bought anew for 2/-"; another "a seine rope" also worth 2s.. Other wills about this time list "pilchard nets" among bequests. This gives credence to the supposition that catches of herring, pilchards and sprats were made by seines hauled on to the beaches of Torquay and Paignton, while "lining" was restricted to the fishermen of Brixham who had few adjacent beaches.

The addition of trawling to this activity enabled the industry to develop extensively so that by about 1850 Brixham was said to have the "largest fishery in England." Meanwhile the infant fisheries on the other side of the Bay remained small by comparison. It has also been suggested that through the purchase of a share in the manorial rights the fishermen of Brixham retained full control over their affairs and eventually, as Eden Phillpotts in *The Haven* explains, "that village under Berry Head within the sheltering arms of Torbay, numbers more lords and ladies of the Manor than any other town in England."

The *Dartmouth Custom House Records*, referred to earlier, give a clear indication of the importance of fishing as long ago as the 1540s. Cargoes of pilchards and herring were being "exported" in large quantities. Salt is also listed frequently. This would have come from the French Atlantic ports and shows that salting, as a means of preservation, was carried out and that local supplies of salt were insufficient. The pressing of fish to produce train or "fish oil" (used for the making of soap) seems to have been done too but must have become uneconomic when huge quantities of cod-oil began to arrive from Newfoundland.

When the Armada ship was brought in it was the Brixham men who helped - a possible indication that even then their boats were larger than those of their neighbours and their superiority as seamen recognised.

Half a century later Brixham folk were much involved in the production of *buckhorn*, strips of whiting cut up by the women, salted, then sun-dried on open ground. It was so called because of the toughness of the finished product. Buckhorn went out from Brixham for a very long time, right up to the coming of the railway to South Devon, when it became possible to get fresh fish to the more distant markets.

The development which put Brixham in the forefront was the introduction of trawl-fishing in the late eighteenth century. The technique of dragging a net "with an open mouth" along the sea-bed to catch the more desirable species had long been known. A petition to Parliament against the practice was made as long ago as the fourteenth century and the controversy had continued over the years, though small beam-trawls may well have been in use before 1700. It is likely that men returning home from the continental wars in the middle of the century brought with them new ideas and stories of how they fished in other countries, so that soon bigger boats with improved sailing characteristics were joining the Brixham fleet. These had the power to pull the heavy trawl-nets along the sea-bottom and choice demersal species like

Brixham breakwater before completion; shipyard on beach (TL)

sole, turbot and plaice were being landed in large quantities.

Coincidentally, the coming of the turnpikes brought a major improvement in roads and thus increased the size of the potential market. London was reached by sending fast cutters to Portsmouth, where the fish was rushed the 72 miles as fast as the horses could run. The South Devon turnpikes provided access to the Exeter and Bath markets soon after.

Facilities at Brixham were inadequate for a growing industry, so in 1799 an Act of Parliament was obtained authorising the construction of a new pier and fish-market. Within four years both were finished. The harbour still needed a breakwater as it was exposed to easterly gales. In 1837 the Quay Lords obtained the necessary authority, and the foundation stone was laid in 1843. Finance was raised by loans and gifts including £319.10s.11d. raised by the inhabitants themselves. The breakwater was designed by James Meadows Rendel (also responsible for the floating-bridge at Dartmouth) but after 1,400 feet had been completed the work stopped for lack of funds.

The inadequate structure was damaged in the Great Hurricane of 1866 and in later storms. Special tolls were authorised in 1875 and application was made to the Government of the day for "convict labour to make Torbay a harbour of refuge."[3] This had the support of major shipowners in Liverpool, London and elsewhere. However, nothing was done until 1909 when a further 600 feet was started with Government help. In 1912 the final thousand feet was begun and the thousand metre Breakwater was opened in September 1916, some 73 years later than hoped. The total cost by then had exceeded £100,000, an early example of "escalating costs". The original £319, raised with such effort, amounted to only a minute fraction of the final overall figure. The oil jetty was added in 1920.

The movement in mid-Victorian times of the fishing smacks to Dover (people there still proudly claim Brixham ancestry) and Ramsgate, and later to Yarmouth and Hull reduced the numbers processing the catches but when they eventually settled there as "colonists" the town lost many of its best fishermen. Evidence to the Royal Commission on Sea Fisheries (Report 1866) noted that only half the fleet remained in Brixham all the year round, a quarter was based permanently in Hull and another ten boats had moved to Ireland. The links with South Wales were forged then too. Brixham school records have many entries for children "gone to Tenby for the fishing" indicating it was then only a temporary migration to the west.

Twenty years later the Fleet went east to fish "during the dull part of the year", which meant that the boats returned to Brixham in July. There were marketing problems as they were forced to dispose of their catches through Lowestoft or London agencies, so the "Torbay Fishing Fleet" was formed to operate from April 1883. Fast cutters were engaged to land the fish quickly. Three admirals were appointed to take duties in turn.

White's Directory of 1850, that invaluable source of information on Victorian Devon, says that Brixham then had 130 smacks. Landings of fish up to 150 tons a week were common and included turbot, sole,

"Ice brigs" in Brixham Harbour

whiting, plaice, mullet, mackerel, flounder and herring. Red mullet was the "pick of the catch" and the most profitable. For many years Brixham had the monopoly but by 1889 there was serious competition from the French and Guernsey trammel fishermen who were getting the delicacy on to the English market earlier than the Brixham men.[4]

The coming of the railway put London just six hours away: almost as soon as the line had opened as far as Torquay a vast quantity of fish was being disposed of: "the prime fish being taken off in light conveyances to the South Devon Railway, the inferior kinds being disposed of in the adjacent villages." For a time there was great prosperity, new vessels were at a premium at a time when the whole community was involved. One of the main difficulties was of course keeping the fish fresh during its journey by rail and about 1860 Arctic ice began to be imported. It was cut from the frozen lakes of Norway, packed in straw, loaded on to fast brigs and brought back to Brixham as quickly as the winds allowed. Certainly the trade was well established by 1869 when the *Dartmouth Chronicle* reported the arrival of *Antelope* with a "cargo of good

Norwegian ice." Three years later she was bringing regular shipments to the Brixham and Torbay Ice Company. An ice-factory was built near Kings Quay in 1900 and for over 20 years black smoke from it poured out over the town as it produced several tons of ice a day. Steam was later replaced by diesel fuel at the ice-plant, but the arrival in the recent past of on-board freezing of catches and other changes made its operation uneconomic. The site is, at the time of writing, cleared for building.

The smacks were a nursery for young seamen; often two of the five man crew (many had only four crew-men including the skipper) were apprentices. A Victorian journalist once posed the question: What about apprentices? It brought the answer:

> They are bound when about fourteen and serve till they reach twenty one. I've got one about nine and a half years with me. His parents are badly off and they wanted rid of him. There's many in that case (position) in Brixham.[5]

Brixham Quay about 1900; ships building and ice-factory working (TL)

Those tan-sailed boats which graced the scene for so long were finally replaced with steam-trawlers, but it took a long time, many would say too long, for them to do so. The sails which attracted the attention of so many artists were that colour because to preserve them they were immersed in a boiling hot concentration of oak-bark, tallow, red and yellow ochre and Stockholm tar.[6] The work was carried out in "barking yards"[7] sited near the Harbour by the crew themselves, the yard being hired out by the day to the smack's owner by the proprietor.

George Parker Bidder, the Moretonhampstead "Calculating Boy" who became a mathematician and engineer in later life, designed the first steam-trawler, which was built experimentally at Dartmouth in 1870, and named the *Bertha* after one of his daughters.[8] Nevertheless, local owners continued to have complete faith in sail. Questioned about the future of steam one replied: "They cost too much to work. There's many that's tried it but they never got on with it." The same spokesman continued: "There was a steam trawler but she hadn't the power to get about. Our smacks would beat her hollow any time." This was wishful thinking: only a short time later there was bitter opposition to steam-powered boats in Brixham "for taking away the markets from our toilers of the deep."[9] By then there were nearly 200 steam vessels at sea, all on the east coast. Although expensive both to build and to operate, they were unaffected by the direction and strength of the wind and so spent less time becalmed or in harbour.

The industry at Brixham also suffered from being dependent on a long railway link to its major markets, which put up costs, the "one barrier keeping this good and wholesome food from the populations of our larger towns." It also lacked access to the large capital sums required to convert the fleet to steam. The sole concession to steam power was the provision of an auxiliary engine which was used to raise the trawl. These were "formerly lifted by turning a long wooden roller, which was worked by men with hand-spikes. The trawls, which it formerly often took 2 hours to raise, are now lifted in 15 minutes."[10]

The men valued their independence. Traditionally they were not paid a weekly wage: their prosperity depended on the success of their fishing - they received a proportionate share of the profits from each trip; the skipper the largest, the "boy" the smallest. (The Department of Employment still designates many Brixham men as "share-fishermen" - with special rights in the Welfare State.)

The womenfolk likewise valued their independence. Fish was auctioned in the market by fisherwomen by Dutch auction, not a common procedure at that time. The catch was arranged in suitable lots and a price named for each portion.[11] Potential buyers would loudly declare other lower ones and the business would continue until a bargain at some intermediate figure was struck. Some of the men, of an enterprising nature, decided to start up on their own and set up in opposition and, like the women, without licences. They were forced to obtain them and demanded that the women did so too. After appeals to authority the men lost the day and the right to trade. As a result a grand celebration was held in the Fish Market where toasts were drunk - in tea. The day ended with "dancing which was kept up with great animation" with "the elder fisherwomen going through the old country dances with marvellous grace and elasticity."

There was another instance of the men's independence of spirit. The *Dartmouth Chronicle* noted that they had "thought fit to follow the

Brixham fishing fleet in port about 1890 (TL)

example set for them in much larger towns - *viz.*- to strike." It concerned a dismissal without notice and was soon settled. The year, surprisingly, was 1860. Thirty years later there was another, this time over "stock-a-bait": shell-fish, crabs and other delicacies found among the main catch which the men and boys were permitted to sell privately. The strikers blockaded the Fish Quay before the affair was settled. Stock-a-bait still provides additional income for the fisherman.

In 1910 there were 213 trawlers of various sizes; 150 men were employed in the three shipyards and nine out of ten boys still went proudly to sea. The War which came just four years later proved to be the turning-point in the industry's fortunes and affected Brixham for a generation. When hostilities broke out, many men joined the Navy as members of the RNR where they manned minesweepers and other small craft. As well as men, vessels were lost by enemy action; at one time six were sunk in one week by U-boats. The Brixham Fleet subsequently went out to fish only under the guard of an armed

Henry Walker's trawlers: the engraver who loved Brixham (courtesy Miss Perks)

steam-trawler.[12] The vessel, which may be said to typify both the sturdiness of the craft and the skills of the crew, was BM291 *Provident*. Skippered by William Pillar, she rescued 71 survivors from HMS *Formidable*, torpedoed in the Channel on 1st January 1915. She was later lost by enemy action. The present-day *Provident* (BM28)[13] owned by the Maritime Trust and based in Devon, has no connection with her illustrious name-sake; she was not built until 1924.

It appears to have been sometime during the 1914-18 War that the three roperies or ropewalks ceased operations. There was Bartlett's at Furzeham, Elliott's on Windmill Hill and a third on Rea Hill.

The returning survivors found out-of-date boats and equipment in a fleet reduced to less than 90.[14] The new fishing grounds were many miles away and the east coast ports were in a more favourable position to benefit. Wrecks in the Channel were causing heavy damage to fishing-gear and there were wealthy men with large yachts willing to pay good wages to experienced seamen. By 1935 there were only 25 boats left; by 1939 little more than a half-dozen. The once famous Fleet was almost extinct. There were however one or two left to join the convoy of

Disused Ropewalk at Windmill Hill, Brixham, about 1920-5

"little ships" which sailed from Brixham on the last day of May 1940 to assist in the evacuation of the British Expeditionary Force from Dunkirk. At least one local man owes his rescue to an unknown Brixham trawler. Until the outbreak of World War II, Torquay was the landing place for large numbers of sprats. Whiting and mackerel were also landed there in more limited quantities.

After 1945 the rebuilding of the fishing industry at Brixham was discussed many times. In 1965 the Brixham fishermen, with the help of local bank managers and business men, formed a cooperative, known as Brixham and Torbay Fish. It now has a membership of 1,100 and an annual turnover of £20 million.[15] Sales of fish have increased thirty-fold since it was founded, and well over half is exported. The Local Authority was responsible for building a new fish-jetty with deep-water facilities which was completed in 1971. An extension is currently projected due to be completed in the Spring of 1987 at an estimated cost of £3.5 million.

IX WRECK AND RESCUE

Torbay has always been sheltered from the prevailing westerlies but occasionally gale force winds blow from the east to produce heavy swells and breakers which pound the beaches and cliffs with great ferocity. Although always a popular anchorage for the British fleet, these easterlies quickly turn the Bay into a boiling cauldron. This is probably why, in 1795, Lord Howe[1] is said to have feared that "Torbay will be the grave of the Navy" when 27 of his ships lost their anchors during a storm. The vulnerability of ships to these winds is sometimes given as one of the reasons why the breakwater at Plymouth was built.

The need for major works to be carried out was recognised as long ago as 1696, as noted earlier, when there were proposals to build a "harbour or mould" from Beacon Point at Torquay. Envisaged to be 550 yards in length it would "contain more than 300 Sail of ships at any time." It was proclaimed that it would be "of extraordinary Service to His Majesty and save the Nation many thousands of pounds *per Annum* in the charge of Victualling the Navy" and that "if at any time a War should happen with *France*, it will prove not only useful to *England* but very injurious to the *French*, it being opposite *St Malo* and but 26 leagues from it .... "

Nothing came of this idea but it was brought up again in the 1860s, when the proposer suggested a breakwater running north-west from Berry Head to Hopes Nose. He explained that there was an unlimited supply of stone on the Head and ample room for a "convict depot should it be thought desirable to carry out the structure by the use of convict labour." The Board of Trade regretted that they had no money available for such work. How different might the situation be now if either of these schemes had come to fruition; however they did not and ships have continued to be wrecked ever since. Both the Lifeboat and the Coastguard Service have effected many rescues, and still do.

Strangely enough it was not stormy when the first major disaster occurred - though the winds rose to gale force later and contributed to the total loss of HMS *Venerable*. In November 1804 the Fleet was ordered to sea just as darkness was falling. During the raising of her anchor a man went overboard and shortly afterwards three men, in one of the boats launched to help him, were lost and drowned though the seamen who had necessitated the rescue in the first place was hauled safely back aboard. In the meantime the great ship had drifted into danger and before long hit the rocks at Roundham between Paignton and Goodrington. The rising sea and increasing swell made rescue difficult but HMS *Goliath*, HMS *Impeteux* and the cutter *Frisk*, at great danger to themselves, took on board many of the crew while others climbed straight onto shore along the bowsprit. When she struck there were 555 men on board but according to a contemporary newspaper only eight were drowned. As this presumably included those lost in the small boat, only five were unaccounted for. There were hints that some of these had not drowned but had deserted. At the court-martial which followed, the captain and crew were honourably acquitted. However one marine, the only one known to have misbehaved, was also court-martialled. He was found guilty and ordered to be "flogged through the Fleet" - his punishment was 200 lashes of the "cat". The people of Paignton received no accolades for their parts in the affair. It was said subsequently that "the conduct of the people on shore was most inhuman, not the slightest assistance was offered .... On the other hand they plundered everything they could reach the next day." Later, detachments of the local Volunteers and Sea Fencibles had to be placed on guard around the wreck.

The Coastguard, originally formed in 1822 to combat the increasing activities of the smugglers, soon began the rescue work for which they are so well-known today. The first awards for bravery at scenes of wrecks were made to serving officers in the Plymouth area as early as the 1820s. Here in Torbay their contributions appear to have been more modest though they must have been involved right from the early days. A Torquay blacksmith named George Gilley achieved local fame by

Coastguard equipment on display in Brixham Museum

The Boxer Rocket was used successfully for many years; two-wheeled carts like this were man-handled by teams of men on the roughest slopes

CRE Company ready for action (Coastguard Museum)

rescuing more than 50 people in his lifetime. On one occasion "by means of a rope he swung off the cliffs of Waldon Hill (now the Terrace Gardens beside the Torbay Road) to reach the schooner *Native* which was stranded on rocks near the Torre Abbey Sands and sent ashore fifteen men and a boy, one at a time, in a basket ...." Gilley must have been an inventive fellow; the "breeches buoy", so similar to a basket, was not invented until 14 years later. The involvement of the Coastguard in this episode appears to have been limited to "furnishing the rope for the basket." They were, however, becoming more and more engaged in rescue from wrecks; their part in this work became so commonplace that contemporary newspapers often dismissed their presence with the curt sentence: "The Coastguard got out their rocket apparatus and worked with a will until all were rescued." The work often involved the back-breaking task of manhandling their rescue equipment for miles up steep cliff-paths in almost impossible weather conditions.

For more than a century the lives of shipwrecked mariners depended on a small team of coastguardsmen supported by volunteers whose only immediate reward was a metal token pressed into their hand at the conclusion of the incident. As late as 1892 it was reported to Parliament that "the lifeboat and the rocket apparatus form the principal means adopted for saving life on the coasts of the United Kingdom." The Report went on to outline the work done by Captain G.W.Manby, inventor of a mortar which projected a line from shore to ships in distress. Various inventors also worked on the use of rockets in place of mortars; finally one was perfected by Colonel Boxer and this became the standard equipment for many years. The Boxer Rocket was successful partly because it was in effect two projectiles, one within the other: when the first had carried to its full elevation, the second fired to carry a line out and over the vessel in distress.

The Manby mortars were operated by the Coastguard from the start but it was not until later, in 1855, that the control of the Stations passed to what was then the Board of Trade. Some of these had rockets, some mortars, some both; a Coastguard Station was established near Paignton Harbour sometime before 1851. The great test of the coastguardsmen's endurance and devotion to duty was to come when the Great Hurricane struck. It is difficult now to appreciate the severity of the storm which hit Torbay on 11th January 1866. Gale-force winds from the south-west accompanied by a snowstorm forced ships to rush for the safety of the Bay. Suddenly however the wind veered to the SSE and within hours over 40 vessels were driven ashore, many of them near Brixham Harbour. It was there that local people, particularly fishermen, performed great acts of heroism dragging seamen from the water. The whole area was cluttered with beams, planks, rigging, sails, barrels, bags of grain and other flotsam which was being cast about in the seething waves. One eye-witness account tells how:

> Private house were converted into temporary refuge and refreshement houses; at the Assembly Room eighty-five seamen were accommodated; the floor covered with straw and on this the poor fellows laid down in rows.[2]

Over at Paignton the *Maria Louisa* had gone on to shore early in the morning and the weighty and cumbersome Manby mortar was manhandled to the Green where "the coastguard attempted to establish communication with the stranded vessel .... but every attempt to throw a line across the rigging failed." This was not surprising as the Manby was notoriously erratic. Subsequently the crew reached the beach by boat. Further around the coast the vessels driven ashore on the more rocky Saltern, Broadsands and Elberry were in much more perilous straits. However:

> Mr Davies, chief boatman at Paignton got the mortar and rocket to Broadsands about two and a half miles over a difficult road and [from] 5 am on that awful morning .... at the risk of their own lives did the good coastguardsmen work until 54 lives had been saved and not one lost of the TEN vessels stranded on their station.[3]

There is an unusual story concerning the eventual demise of the Boxer Rocket. It was not until some time after the end of World War II that it was superseded because it was believed by some officers to be

109

The Great Storm 1866 Wrecked ships at Brixham (TL)

erratic in operation. After complaints it was found that those in use had been made by one man for over 40 years and that he had died without disclosing the full secrets of its manufacture. Rockets of modern design for life-saving are still issued by the Department of Transport to Coast Rescue Companies but they are needed less and less nowadays. Helicopters, in this area mainly from Culdrose and Chivenor, have brought a new dimension to rescue at sea, for they can hover in near impossible conditions while winchmen hoist casualties from equally impossible situations.

Modern rescue equipment does not of course in any way detract from the exceptional work done by the lifeboats of the Royal National Lifeboat Institution. Despite the known importance of Torbay as a place of refuge during storms there does not seem to have been any pressure applied to having a lifeboat stationed there. Possibly it was thought that the one at Teignmouth was sufficient but the Great Storm proved it to be totally ineffective. As soon as its severity was appreciated the boat was sent for, but the seas were so bad that it was unable to clear the bar. It was then loaded on its transporting carriage and drawn by teams of horses over Shaldon Bridge, along the Turnpike road and eventually to Torquay harbour. By the time it was launched from the slipway the period of greatest danger was over; however it was in time to save seven people from two vessels still in trouble.

The RNLI quickly organised a local Committee and set about enrolling crew-members. In the meantime a group of Exeter people started their own Lifeboat Fund and soon collected £600 which they passed to the Institution for a Torbay station. Matters went so well it was hoped that the vessel, to be named appropriately the *City of Exeter*, would be ready by October. It was however decided, on expert advice, to locate the new lifeboat, not at Torquay but at Brixham, where it was likely to be of more value. By doing so its launch was delayed as there was an outbreak of cholera in the town.

The first four Brixham lifeboats (known as the Torbay Lifeboats from 1924) were of course pulled mainly by oarsmen, and it was not until 1922 that the first motor-powered lifeboat, the *Alfred and Clara Heath*, arrived in South Devon. The engine for this boat had been built with a legacy, and somewhat unusually, was formally named *Mary and Katherine* at the inaugural ceremony. The *George Shee* was in service throughout the 1930s and during World War II. Among her launches were three to United States Army landing-craft in trouble during preparations for D-Day. Her successor, the *Princess Alexandra of Kent*, was a familiar sight as she lay at her moorings in the Outer Harbour at Brixham during the sixties and early seventies. Torbay Lifeboat is, at the time of writing, the *Edward Brydges*, a fast 54-foot vessel with the latest navigational and life-saving equipment. A far cry indeed from that first 34-foot, ten-oared self-righter. This was kept in a house built near Bolton Cross in the town centre, because from there it could be taken on its own carriage along Fore Street to the Harbour, or by road to launching spots to north and south, which may have been more practicable in very hazardous weather conditions. Since her first service at sea in March 1869 the Torbay Lifeboat has gone out over 600 times. Her proud record is fully documented.[4]

It may seem strange that in spite of the decision to station the Torbay vessel at Brixham there should have been a meeting in Torquay only nine years later which petitioned the RNLI to give another boat. Rather surprisingly this was agreed, and in May 1876 the *Mary Brundrett* arrived and was hauled on her carriage amid great rejoicing through the streets of Torquay to the new lifeboat station built at the Ladies Bathing Cove (now Beacon Cove behind Coral Island). This was the only possible site, on land given by the lord of the manor Sir Lawrence Palk. The carriage was so designed that the lifeboat could also be launched from either Paignton or Babbacombe.[5]

The arrival of motor-power at Brixham with promises of increased range and a faster service meant that the Torquay lifeboat was no longer needed. It ceased operations in March 1923. The *Wighton*, the third on the station, was sold for conversion to a yacht. The building became a Torquay Corporation café for over 50 years, until it was demolished during redevelopment of the area.

It is not widely known that in 1917 Mr William Ball presented a small 20 foot ship's lifeboat for inshore rescues around Torquay Harbour. This action perhaps foreshadowed the introduction of the small inshore rescue craft which have become so well known around the British coasts in the 1980s. The BBC's *Blue Peter* programme has done much to maintain this newer, but still voluntary, service. Except for some full-time mechanics who are paid, all RNLI crews are volunteers, and there are always more men at hand when the distress maroons are fired than are needed. Unfortunately for sightseers at Brixham harbour, the modern technology of "bleepers" has made the muffled explosion which used to summon the coxswain and his crew unnecessary. They still run "at the double" because launches demand the same urgency as they always have.

X TWENTIETH CENTURY TORBAY

When the present century dawned, the British Empire was at its strongest. Dominance was maintained on the Seven Seas by a powerful Royal Navy. The enemy in any future war was now likely to be Germany, which had started a huge naval expansion in furtherance of her world-wide trading ventures. The Channel Fleet was seen in Torbay each summer; for instance in 1905 "113 ships of war, the largest assemblage on record," were at anchor: two years later it was the Home Fleet, which included the first appearance of a new class of capital ship, HMS *Dreadnought*.

There was another important visitor that year. In August 1907 the Antarctic Exploration vessel *Nimrod* was moored in Torquay Harbour overnight before sailing for New Zealand prior to moving into the southern polar region. The leader of the expedition, Lieutenant Ernest Shackleton RN, remained in the town, staying at the Knoll in Torquay until the end of October.

"The Miracle of the Aeroplane" *Daily Mail*
In July 1910 a south-westerly gale in Mounts Bay, Cornwall forced the transfer of the imminent Review of the Fleet by George V to Torbay at a day's notice. The arrival of the ships brought an estimated 20,000 spectators to view the 37 battleships, 27 cruisers and the many other smaller men-of-war, some 200 in all, which were assembling in lines across the Bay. While most had to watch from vantage-points the more privileged members of contemporary society were able to see the events unfold at closer quarters. The Hon. Winifred Norbury wrote:

Preparing for the flight in Torre Abbey meadows (TL)

Grahame White flying over the Fleet, July 1910 (Part of a contemporary postcard)

Amateur photographer's view of the flight with the Royal Yacht Victoria and Albert *steaming ahead (TL)*

.... after luncheon we all proceeded forth at 2.15 with the intention of going round the Fleet in a steamer. We got down in good time for the 3 o'c. one and got good places on board and were taken a nice, long, round in and out among the ships & just as we were getting back to harbour the guns began firing the salute and we could see the Royal Yacht in the distance. It was most thrilling and the guns were splendid. Cousin Mary and I fortunately both decided we did not wish to leave our Steamer but would go round again in the next trip so we sent the maids off and mounted into one of the boats which were on the top of the Steamer and had a much better view .... When we reached harbour again the *Victoria & Albert* had just come up through the whole Fleet and we saw her moored .... The King and Queen were visible on a high platform and people with glasses could see them distinctly but we were too far off to be able to do that .... Mr Graham White the next excitement after the Royal Yacht has arrived but cannot fly this evening (because of the weather).[1]

That last short sentence is all Winifred Norbury considered necessary to record an event which would be one of the most momentous in Torbay's maritime history.

Mr White, the owner of a fragile wood-and-canvas aeroplane was determined to demonstrate to the Admiral of the Fleet the King "the utility of the flying-machine in the naval warfare of the future." When the forced transfer took place White first announced his intention of flying from Cornwall to Torquay but he eventually travelled with his plane to Newton Abbot by train and instead of coming the last six miles by air the Farman biplane was brought into a field (now the Abbey Gardens) "at the bottom of Belgrave Road fronting Belgrave Hotel, to remain under police protection so that it would be ready for a flight over the war-vessels in the bay."

The Fleet was due to leave its anchorage between eight and nine o'clock to exercise in the Channel, but dawn broke with the ships almost totally enveloped in a thick haze. Any of the projected manoeuvres would have been a hazardous undertaking in such conditions. The weather, however, improved about noon and the sun shone fitfully. Shortly after one o'clock Grahame White "ascended his seat", his mechanic started the seven-cylinder Gnome engine and he commenced his take-off uphill rising in the air "like a horse at a fence and was up and over the royal yacht in a flash." He made two flights over the Fleet, the first in the early afternoon when he "exhibited the possibilities of the aeroplane in attack; the second in the evening when he showed its use for defence against invading warships." On this occasion he reached a height of some 1,500 feet.

The *Daily Mail* told its readers the next day how Mr White had given the King and Queen "an unforgettable thrill which comes with the first sight of the miracle of an aeroplane in flight." The Mail concluded:

> The heavy broadsides of the super-Dreadnoughts were helpless and ineffective against him. Not a single gun could be elevated to an angle that could reach him. Laden with a supposed cargo of the as yet uninvented X-power explosive which the advent of the aeroplane renders inevitable, he had £100,000,000 worth of the British Navy helpless beneath him, caught in the narrow waters of the enclosed bay.

How prophetic the newspaper proved to be. It was only a little over 31 years later that the Japanese were destroying a great United States battle-fleet in Pearl Harbour almost exactly as forecast.

The arrival of steam and the rapid growth of an overseas merchant shipping industry encouraged entrepreneurs to look to Torbay for additional revenue. Among these was the Denaby and Cadeby Colliery Company which was granted permission to anchor a coal hulk near the end of Brixham breakwater. From the number calling for bunkering (722 in 1912-13) this facility must have been used mainly by vessels on passage. The hulks were old sailing-ships with their hulls gutted and derricks attached to fore- and main-masts; from time to time they were seen against the quay at Torquay, presumably for their fuel stocks to be replenished. The *London City* was used for coal-bunkering throughout the 1930s, moored to landward of the oil jetty in Brixham outer harbour.

Land battles in the 1914-18 War were fought far away, but sea-warfare, mainly through the U-boat menace, reached the very

117

"Denaby and Cadeby Main Collieries" coal-hulk at quayside; coastal steam-vessel, possibly Coastlines at Beacon Quay, Torquay (TL)

fringes of the Bay as ships were mined, torpedoed or sunk by gunfire. Torquay harbour became a small naval base when minesweepers and patrol-boats were located there. In 1917 a depot was established by ladies of the local gentry to provide comforts for the crews and for those based at Dartmouth as well.[2]

The Coastlines Ltd. shed in Beacon Quay was adapted and used by the Royal Navy Air Service as a seaplane hanger. The Short Brothers 184 aircraft were lifted in and out of the water by cranes and went on patrol, taking off from the open sea near Haldon Pier after taxiing through the harbour entrance. After the merging of the Royal Naval Air Service and the Royal Flying Corps in April 1918 the Coastlines shed became a Royal Air Force station with 239 Squadron based there. Soon after the Armistice a German mine-laying submarine, U161, accompanied by a British minesweeper and other boats, arrived and was open to inspection. The RAF played its part in the extravaganza - the ships "fired guns, sounded hooters, and flew flags while waterplanes flew in

the air, descended on the water and generally made things look lively."
The submarine was on view during the week before Christmas 1918 and
so the 13 men on board were invited to the Sailors' Rest "for a good
supper which they enjoyed. A charming impromptu concert followed."
The Squadron left Torquay in May 1919.

In the aftermath of that War two German torpedo-boats being towed
to the breakers went ashore at Paignton. The Coastguard Rescue
Company there attended the casualties and in the "Rewards for 1920",
George Pearce, Enrolled Volunteer, received "£1 in addition to other
allowances" for "going over the rocks and through the surf .... with
lifelines by which the crew of three men were rescued." Two regular
Coastguards received only 10/- for a similar rescue at the other
location.[3]

Between the Wars

The Navy was again a regular visitor in the 1920s. In July 1922 "our
sailor King" arrived in Torbay to inspect the 70-odd vessels in the
Atlantic Fleet. "Not since pre-war days has the great might of Britain's

Between the Wars; ships of the Fleet in Torbay, 1934 (TL)

Senior Service stretched itself across this famous watering-place. Hundreds of excited and patriotic spectators assembled", wrote a journalist of the day. Although over 250 warships had been lost during World War I, Britain ended it with nearly twice the tonnage it had in 1914, and many of the replacements were in the Fleet which raised anchor and sailed out to meet the *Victoria and Albert* which was steaming down from Portsmouth. The ships arrived back in one magnificent procession in line-astern with the Royal Yacht at its head. They fanned out to anchor in long lines across the Bay towards Brixham with the King's yacht just off Haldon Pier.

In 1924 a large Fleet lay in Torbay prior to sailing off to the Spithead Review. Now grown to over 80 major vessels, it included those capital ships with household names which were to be lost in World War II with so many of their crews: *Barham*, *Warspite*, *Valiant*, *Royal Oak*, *Royal Sovereign* and *Revenge*. An event of historical importance to the Service took place on the quarter-deck of the *Queen Elizabeth*: 500 officers from the ships of the fleet, including all the admirals and captains, attended a farewell At Home on board. A major reorganisation of the Navy followed the Review.

The July visits remained an annual event. Hundreds of blue-jackets and marines landed nightly from picket-boats and tenders for a short break ashore. They were busy days for the volunteer helpers at the Torquay Sailors Rest which had been set up in 1902 and opened officially a year later by Miss "Aggie" Weston, the "Sailors' Friend".

Coasters for Work and Racers for Pleasure
As well as naval vessels there were civilian visitors to the coast. General cargoes were brought in for Coastlines Ltd., usually in their own ships, on a regular service which started in the Port of London and ended in Swansea or some other South Wales port. Coastlines had their own warehouse on Beacon Quay at Torquay, which had reverted to its former appearance after the sea-planes left. The round trip for the coasters took about a fortnight and the part-cargoes unloaded included wool (for Newton Abbot) and potatoes from Spain, Jersey and Scotland. Cement, mostly in Blue Circle's own ships, came from London and there was timber from Sweden and Norway. Coal-ships

Sand-barge Mizpah *at Torquay about 1934*

Coaster "Charlus" and timber-carrying three-master at Beacon Quay, Torquay in about 1934

displaying large banners on their bridges or amidships proclaimed they had Renwick's Coals on board. Stacks of timber left for a day or so on Haldon Pier or Beacon Quay displayed boards saying "Thomas Crossman"; these cargoes arrived in both steam vessels and elegant sailing ships, most with northern European ports-of-registry. Little of this trade revived after the 1939-45 War.

The years of the last decade before that War were the last great period of the gentlemen-yachtsmen. Bunting fluttered around all the harbours at Regatta-time but it was at Torquay that vessels and crew assembled in the largest numbers. Steam yachts were moored in the outer harbour, many dressed overall. One of the most graceful was Lord Runciman's schooner *Sunbeam II* entered in Torquay harbourmaster's dues book in 1933 as being of 658 tons, twice the size of the present-day Sail Training Association's *Sir Winston Churchill* and *Malcolm Miller*. They each demand a crew of three dozen or more; Sunbeam would have needed at least a similar number.

Torquay Royal Regatta; ships dressed overall, August 1898 (TL)

Luxury yachts in Torquay Harbour about 1930 (TL)

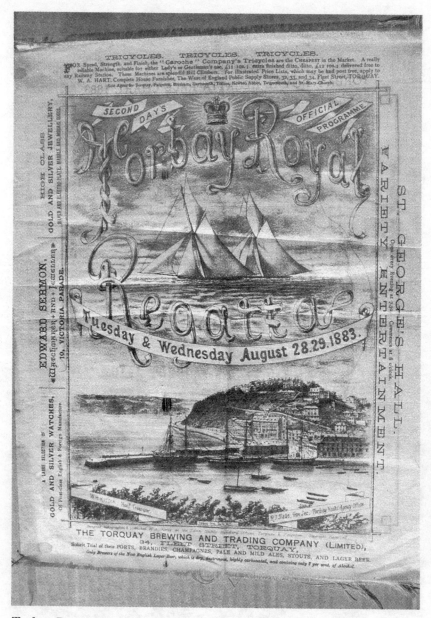

Torbay Royal Regatta; programme on silk, 1883

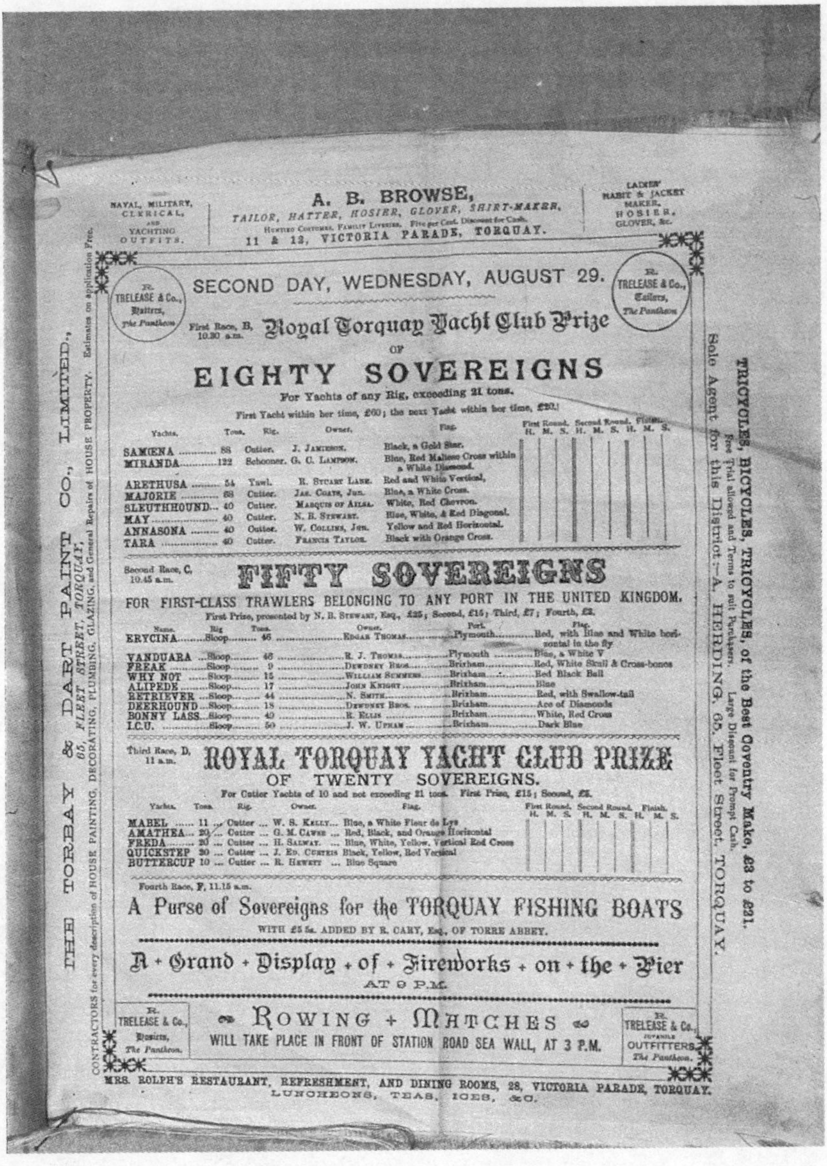

NAVAL, MILITARY, CLERICAL, AND YACHTING OUTFITS.

A. B. BROWSE,
TAILOR, HATTER, HOSIER, GLOVER, SHIRT-MAKER,
Hunting Costumes, Family Liveries. Five per Cent. Discount for Cash.
11 & 13, VICTORIA PARADE, TORQUAY.

LADIES' HABIT & JACKET MAKER, HOSIER, GLOVER, &c.

R. TRELEASE & Co., Hatters, The Pantheon

R. TRELEASE & Co., Tailors, The Pantheon

THE TORBAY & DART PAINT CO., LIMITED, 65, *FLEET STREET, TORQUAY;* CONTRACTORS for every description of HOUSE PAINTING, DECORATING, PLUMBING, GLAZING, and General Repairs of HOUSE PROPERTY. Estimates on application Free.

TRICYCLES, BICYCLES, TRICYCLES, of the Best Coventry Make, £3 to £21. Free Trial allowed and Terms to suit Purchasers. Large Discount for Prompt Cash. Sole Agent for this District:—A. HERDING, 65, Fleet Street, TORQUAY.

SECOND DAY, WEDNESDAY, AUGUST 29.

First Race, B, 10.30 a.m.

Royal Torquay Yacht Club Prize OF EIGHTY SOVEREIGNS

For Yachts of any Rig, exceeding 21 tons.

First Yacht within her time, £60; the next Yacht within her time, £20.

Yachts.	Tons.	Rig.	Owner.	Flag.	First Round. H. M. S.	Second Round. H. M. S.	Finish. H. M. S.
SAMŒNA	88	Cutter.	J. Jamieson.	Black, a Gold Star.			
MIRANDA	122	Schooner.	G. C. Lampson.	Blue, Red Maltese Cross within a White Diamond.			
ARETHUSA	54	Yawl.	R. Stuart Lane.	Red and White Vertical.			
MAJORIE	68	Cutter.	Jas. Coats, Jun.	Blue, a White Cross.			
SLEUTHHOUND	40	Cutter.	Marquis of Ailsa.	White, Red Chevron.			
MAY	40	Cutter.	N. B. Stewart.	Blue, White, & Red Diagonal.			
ANNASONA	40	Cutter.	W. Collins, Jun.	Yellow and Red Horizontal.			
TARA	40	Cutter.	Francis Taylor.	Black with Orange Cross.			

Second Race, C, 10.45 a.m.

FIFTY SOVEREIGNS

FOR FIRST-CLASS TRAWLERS BELONGING TO ANY PORT IN THE UNITED KINGDOM.

First Prize, presented by N. B. Stewart, Esq., £25; Second, £15; Third, £7; Fourth, £3.

Name.	Rig.	Tons.	Owner.	Port.	Flag.
ERYCINA	Sloop	46	Edgar Thomas	Plymouth	Red, with Blue and White horizontal in the fly
VANDUARA	Sloop	46	R. J. Thomas	Plymouth	Blue, a White V
FREAK	Sloop	9	Dewdney Bros.	Brixham	Red, White Skull & Cross-bones
WHY NOT	Sloop	15	William Summers	Brixham	Red Black Ball
ALIPEDE	Sloop	17	John Knight	Brixham	Blue
RETRIEVER	Sloop	44	N. Smith	Brixham	Red, with Swallow-tail
DEERHOUND	Sloop	18	Dewdney Bros.	Brixham	Ace of Diamonds
BONNY LASS	Sloop	40	R. Ellis	Brixham	White, Red Cross
I.C.U.	Sloop	50	J. W. Upham	Brixham	Dark Blue

Third Race, D, 11 a.m.

ROYAL TORQUAY YACHT CLUB PRIZE OF TWENTY SOVEREIGNS.

For Cutter Yachts of 10 and not exceeding 21 tons. First Prize, £15; Second, £5.

Yachts.	Tons.	Rig.	Owner.	Flag.	First Round. H. M. S.	Second Round. H. M. S.	Finish. H. M. S.
MABEL	11	Cutter	W. S. Kelly	Blue, a White Fleur de Lys			
AMATHEA	20	Cutter	G. M. Cawse	Red, Black, and Orange Horizontal			
FREDA	20	Cutter	H. Salway.	Blue, White, Yellow, Vertical Red Cross			
QUICKSTEP	20	Cutter	J. Ed. Curteis	Black, Yellow, Red Vertical			
BUTTERCUP	10	Cutter	R. Hewett	Blue Square			

Fourth Race, F, 11.15 a.m.

A Purse of Sovereigns for the TORQUAY FISHING BOATS

WITH £5 5s. ADDED BY R. CARY, Esq., OF TORRE ABBEY.

A Grand Display of Fireworks on the Pier

AT 9 P.M.

ROWING MATCHES

WILL TAKE PLACE IN FRONT OF STATION ROAD SEA WALL, AT 3 P.M.

R. TRELEASE & Co., Hosiers, The Pantheon.

R. TRELEASE & Co., JUVENILE OUTFITTERS, The Pantheon.

MRS. ROLPH'S RESTAURANT, REFRESHMENT, AND DINING ROOMS, 28, VICTORIA PARADE, TORQUAY.
LUNCHEONS, TEAS, ICES, &C.

TALL SHIPS IN TORBAY

Though the smaller classes were well represented too, the great attraction was the contest between the large "J" class yachts, Fabulously expensive to build and race, they included King George V's *Britannia* (until she was sunk after his death in 1935), *Velsheda*, *Shamrock*, *Astra*, *Candida* and *Endeavour*. The last named vessel was to challenge unsuccessfully for the America's Cup in 1934, as did her successor *Endeavour II* in 1937. Both sailed in Torbay. Some 20 years before, in July 1914, an earlier challenger, *Shamrock*, had called in on her way to the United States. Because of the Great War this contest was cancelled. These huge and graceful craft raced around the course, "their slim bows cutting through the water; their lee-decks awash with the crisp clear foam to the delight of the great crowds of sightseers who thronged Daddyhole Plain, Haldon Pier and other vantage points." The smaller yachts have proliferated vastly in numbers over the years since then but in spite of the ornamental spinnakers they sport in a following wind have never replaced the magnificent grandeur of the "J's".

The Annual Boat Race mentioned briefly earlier has developed over the 120-year period to become the Torbay Royal Regatta, which of course continues to be held annually. The first recorded Race took place in 1811 but for some reason the official commencement of the event has always been taken as 1813, possibly because that year cups and prizes to the value of 20 guineas were offered.[4] There were two classes of entrant; for "gentlemen's boats" the entrance fee was five shillings; "Other boats, Two shillings and sixpence." The following year it was emphasised that the first class should be sailed only by yachts "the real property of reputed Gentlemen only."

The word "Regatta" first appears on a cup raced for and won by *Belle Savage* in 1825. Another important year was 1828 when the Duchess of Clarence, later Queen Consort of King William IV, was in Torquay and the town was full of "fashionables". Royalty were in the Bay again when the Duchess of Kent and the young Princess Victoria arrived in the yacht *Emerald* and stayed overnight in the Royal Hotel. In 1839 Victoria, the new Queen, granted royal patronage to what was then still called Torquay Regatta. Many successful regattas have been held over the years; fireworks appear to have been introduced in 1836 and the fair on the Quay became an added attraction about 1841. The Torbay Yacht

Club was founded in 1863 with Sir Lawrence Palk, Bart., as the first Commodore; it became the Royal Torbay Yacht Club in 1875.[5] Other yacht and sailing clubs in the Torbay towns now offer opportunities for residents and visitors to sail in competition and for pleasure; some members compete internationally.

World War II and the Americans

Torbay remained a popular summer rendezvous for the Navy right up to the outbreak of war in 1939 but soon all ships were based in places where booms could be laid to keep German U-Boats at bay. The first local result was that early in September the beaches became thronged with men, young and old, filling vast numbers of sandbags to protect public and other buildings. The German *blitzkrieg* across Europe and the speedy occupation of the Channel coast completely changed the situation. The threat of invasion meant that pill-boxes were built in strategic positions, barbed wire and mines laid, and anti-tank barriers constructed ready to be set into place when the enemy landed. Heavy gun-batteries were built at Brixham and on Corbyn Head: the concrete emplacements can still be seen in Battery Gardens, but the naval guns at Livermead were taken away soon after a serious accident in which several Home Guards were killed.

When emergency calls were sent out along the south and east coasts on 30th May 1940 for "little ships" to assist in the evacuation of the BEF from Dunkirk, many along this coast responded, and about a dozen set out from Brixham the next day. Some were so slow and were so long en route that they arrived too late to take part.

Later in the War the RAF's No 39 Air-Sea Rescue unit, with high-speed launches, was based in Torquay Harbour (one is believed to have suffered damage to her stern when she hit a mine). It was however at Brixham that major contributions were made to the war effort. Over a thousand vessels were built or repaired at Upham's shipyard. The Central Diving School of HMS *Vernon*, which was transferred to the town, trained "frogmen" and other specialists in underwater operations who were then deployed in Normandy, the south of France and elsewhere.[6]

From time to time there were indications that German E-Boats were operating against Allied shipping in the vicinity. The only documented occasion however, was when a small German flotilla evaded HMS *Hawkins*, the British warship controlling Exercise Tiger at the Slapton Sands battle area, and attacked the assault ships. At least two landing-craft were sunk, killing many United States servicemen.[7]

Preparing for D-Day; Brixham in late May 1944 (US official photograph)

The decision of the Allies to create a Second Front by breaching the Nazis' Atlantic Wall brought the Americans to the south-west of England. In preparation for Operation Overlord hundreds of thousands of US Army troops poured into the area between Weymouth and Land's End for training, billeting and eventual embarkation. Two great assault forces were assembled, code-named "U" and "O" (they later landed in Normandy on Utah and Omaha beaches) and it was troops for the former who were concentrated around Salcombe, Dartmouth and Torbay. Training was to be carried out under battle conditions with live ammunition so, soon after the arrival of the advance parties in November 1943, the evacuation of the South Hams was under way. This is not part of the Torbay story. Some training was however done in the Bay. Among the histories written in the USA is one by Selby Hardenbergh of the 460th Amphibian Truck Company equipped with DUKWs (familiarly known as "Ducks"). This unit arrived in Paignton in January 1944. Local people must have watched these lumbering craft rounding Roundham Head; they embarked on Paignton beach and "wet-landed" at Goodrington and Broadsands.

Later, in the Spring of 1944, the British War Government made the whole coastal belt some ten miles in depth "a protected area from April 1st until further notice"; this stretched from the Wash to Land's End. Non-residents were prohibited from entering and people were instructed to carry identity cards at all times. Local newspapers reported the story of one Fleming Kent who received 14 days' imprisonment for being in Camborne, "a protected area without permission." He was apparently only giving corn-cob and pumpkins to the local GIs. If this was intended to discourage "incomers" the Torquay magistrates were equally severe with residents; Mrs Leigh was fined £20 with five guineas costs for "communicating to another person information which may or may not be useful to an enemy." The censor who opened her letter, and no doubt all others, found that she had told her son about military equipment near the place where he was contemplating staying. Warnings were issued to future transgressors that it would be imprisonment "without the option of a fine."

In the harbours at both Brixham and Torquay, concrete "hards" were built down which tanks and other fighting vehicles could be loaded into LSTs (landing ship-tanks). Temporary piers were also erected for embarking soldiers onto Assault Ships. At Brixham shortly before D-Day three houses in Berry Head Road were requisitioned at five days' notice before being demolished so that the US Army's huge tanks and support vehicles could negotiate the sharp turn near the present Lifeboat Station.

On 29th May 1944 the German News Agency broadcast that:

> Torquay was the objective of last night's raid on Britain. Formations of heavy German bombers dropped large numbers of incendiary bombs on the harbour installations which had been lit up by flares. Quays and warehouses were also bombed.

TALL SHIPS IN TORBAY

World War II storm in Torquay; there were many barbed wire defences and the gun-battery on Corbyn Head is visible under camouflage nets

This was reported without comment in a local newspaper - censorship allowed no more. Some damage was done and civilian lives lost. In spite of this and other attacks the German High Command remained unaware of the precise date of the invasion and the many thousand troops embarked without incident on to the many ships lying in the Bay. In turn they waited to enter the two small harbours to load their heavy cargoes; others received complements of foot-troops who shinned up ladders and nets to get aboard. All public transport stopped as tanks, personnel-carriers and the paraphernalia of the modern US Army queued nose-to-tail on the Brixham road and on the sea-front approaches to Torquay harbour. The narrow streets rang to the sound of infantry marching three abreast in battle dress and with full equipment.

It is now a fact of history that the invasion of Europe was a success. An invasion of Torbay was soon to take place on 11th July the coast ban was lifted and for the first time in five years the beaches of Torbay were open to visitors. "We expect a big rush of holidaymakers to the South West" said the GWR. Because of the War there were no extra trains and London was still being menaced by the V-weapons. It was in July too that the barbed wire barriers to the sands at Paignton were being removed so it must have been a desolate scene which greeted the visitors, who had to share the seashore with the large number of evacuees, over 2,000, who had just arrived to escape the flying-bombs. Paignton Pier was out of action: a large section near the sands had been dismantled to prevent its use by the invading Germans.

The Last Four Decades
When considering recent history there are two choices; either to record all that has happened or to limit the narrative to those events which may have some significance for the future. The second is chosen here.

As the country was still returning to normal after World War II, the 1948 Olympic Games were held in London. The prestigious yachting events took place on circular courses set out across Torbay. After the opening ceremony in front of Torre Abbey the Olympic flame burned on the mansion house balcony, but the centre of operations moved to the Marine Spa (now demolished) which became the headquarters where the yachtsmen and journalists from 25 nations gathered. A large water-tank, not unlike those which had recently stood in many British cities for use against fire-bomb attacks, was built on Beacon Quay. In this all the competing yachts were rigidly measured and tested. The races took place on three courses where 6-metres, Stars, Dragons, Swallows and Fireflies battled for the medals; there was just one Gold for Britain.

In July 1956, 21 vessels set out on what was officially called the "Torbay to Lisbon International Sail-Training Race."[8] For many people looking across the Bay, it was the first time that they had seen square-rigged ships under full sail. The large ships included the three-masted Portuguese barque *Sagres*, the Norwegian *Sorlandet* and a modern Danish vessel the *Georg Stage*. There were smaller ones as well: the *Artica II* from Italy was only 16 tons. The overall winner was the British ketch *Moyana*. Sadly she sank off the Lizard on the return voyage, but without loss of life.

TALL SHIPS IN TORBAY

By 1962 when the race again started from Torbay with Rotterdam the destination, it had been christened the Tall Ships Race. It has continued from different locations to distant foreign ports at intervals ever since. "Tall Ships" present one of the great sea-spectacles of our time.

Only a few months after that first race to Lisbon another piece of maritime history reached fruition when the replica *Mayflower II* was launched from Upham's Yard in Brixham in September.[9] builder Stuart Upham the opportunity to use tools similar to those which had created the seventeenth century original: adzes, axes, gimbletts (for boring holes), rasps (for shaping wood) and many others. The oak tree needed for the main stem was one of the biggest to be found in Britain at the time, being over six feet in circumference and, of course, from Devonshire. Another great oak block was needed for the keel. Planking was fastened to the frames with wooden treenails - just as on the first *Mayflower*. Wood for treenails must be dry and seasoned so those used were made from 150 year old Devon cider casks. Her sails were made by Harold Bridge, said then to be the last master sail-maker in the town; he had learned his trade making sails for the old Brixham trawlers. Commander Alan Villiers was master for the voyage, which attracted world-wide attention. *Mayflower II* passed south of Cape Cod on 12th June 1957 having successfully crossed the Atlantic just as her predecessor had done three and a half centuries earlier.

Ships taking part in NATO exercises slip in and out of the Bay in small numbers. The last great gathering, possibly the last ever, of British warships took place in July 1969 when the Queen, with the Duke of Edinburgh, reviewed the Western Fleet assembled off Daddyhole Plain from the deck of HMY *Britannia*. Nearly 40 vessels were at anchor when the Fleet received its new Colours from Her Majesty in a ceremony held on the flight-deck of HMS *Eagle*. As a sign of changing times in the Royal Navy the event was followed by a fly-past of 89 helicopters and aircraft of the Fleet Air Arm. Thousands lined Torbay to watch.

In the last decade the demand for oil in the west has brought many oil tankers to the pilot station "one mile north east of Berry Head." Some of these have been VLCCs (very large crude carriers) of a half million tonnes deadweight and more. Lightening operations (to reduce the draught of these huge floating "bath-tubs") take place in neighbouring Lyme Bay to the north. Concern about possible oil-spillages there have prompted some to warn that the ecology and marine life of Torbay could be irreparably damaged at any time. The *Torrey Canyon* affair remains fresh in people's minds, and the minor loss of only ten tonnes of crude from the *Hemithrocus* in 1975 did nothing to calm these fears. Earlier, in 1970, crowds gathered to watch the *Pacific Glory*, which had been seriously damaged by fire after a collision further east, having some of the remaining oil pumped from her scarred and twisted hull. The most worrying incident occurred only a year later when the *Trinity Navigator* (only 42,800 tonnes and a midget compared with today's mammoths) went ashore fully-laden north of Berry Head and was only freed through the skill of a local pilot, Captain Bob Curtis. There was dismay at the time that the Liberian-registered vessel was sailing with her radar unserviceable and her Chinese master "had only a very slight command of the English language." Elaborate emergency plans have been prepared and the specialised equipment now at hand will, it is hoped, prevent a future major disaster.

As the century draws towards its end travel has moved away from the sea into the clouds and it seems that any future war will be fought among the stars; Torbay's future is with flotillas of "little ships" - for pleasure.

Notes to the text

Chapter I
1 Brixey, A. *Story of Torbay*, p.19
2 Hoskins, W.G. *Devon*, p.45
3 Seymour, D.J. *Torre Abbey*, p.82
4 Brixey, op.cit., p.28
5 Oppenheim, M. *Maritime History of Devon*, p.20
6 ibid, p.21
7 *Torquay Directory*, 14 Nov. 1923
8 Brixey, op.cit., p.33
9 ibid., p.34
10 *Torquay Directory* 12 Jan. 1887
11 ibid., 20 Mar. 1918
12 ibid., 28 Mar. 1928

Chapter II
1 Oppenheim, op.cit., p.31
2 Williams, N.L. *Sir Walter Raleigh*
3 Brixey, op.cit., p.41
4 Oppenheim, op.cit., p.52
5 *See* Bibliography
6 *Trans. Devon. Assoc.*, v.88, 1956, pp.90–101
7 Russell, P. *Dartmouth*, Chap.IV
8 Brixey, op.cit., p.52
9 *Trans. Devon. Assoc.*, v.115, 1983, pp.19–36
10 ibid., v.39, 1907, pp.168–9

Chapter III
1 Oppenheim, op.cit., p.52
2 Russell *History of Torquay*, p.33
3 Oppenheim, op.cit., p.55
4 Brixey, op.cit., p.50
5 Camden Society, *Camden Miscellany*, v.17, pp.v.ff
6 Dymond, R. & White, J.T. *A Chronological Record*, p.15
7 Dymond and White, op.cit., pp.15–19
8 Russell, op.cit., p.35
9 Brixey, op.cit., p.60
10 Clowes: *History of the Navy*, v.2, p.323
11 Clowes: ibid., v.2, p.235
12 N.N.: *Expedition of the Highness the Prince of Orange: written at Wincanton*, 1688
13 Whittle, J. *An exact diary of the late expedition of His Illustrious Highness the Prince of Orange*, 1689

Chapter IV
1 Thomas, F. *Humorous and other poetic pictures*, p.100
2 Rattenbury, J. *Memoirs of a smuggler*, pp.57–61
3 Norway, Arthur H. *Highways and Byways in Devon and Cornwall*, p.65
4 Larn, R. *Devon Shipwrecks*, p.100

NOTES

Chapter V   1   Russell, P. *Torquay*, p.59
2   Original in Torre Abbey Art Gallery
3   Brixey, op.cit., p.69
4   White, J.T., *History of Torquay*, p.98
5   Russell, op.cit., pp.41–5
6   Oppenheim, op.cit., p.111
7   ibid., p.113
8   Dymond, R. & White, J. op.cit., pp.15–19
9   Brixey, op.cit., p.75
10   Larn, op.cit., p.102
11   From William Winget's scrapbook in Torquay Museum
12   Torquay Directory, 9 Oct. 1912
13   White, op.cit., p.142ff
14   *The News*, 13 Aug.1815

Chapter VI   1   State Papers Supplementary Bundle 136, No.249
2   Journal of the Comm. for Trade and Plantations 1776, p.177
3   Clowes, W. op.cit., v.4, p.156
4   Trotter, T. *Medicina Nautica*, v.1, p.45
5   Robinson, Charles H. *British Tar in Fact and Fiction*, 1968
6   Russell, P. op.cit., p.51
7   Trotter, op.cit., v.1, p.37
8   Clowes, op.cit., v.7, p.73
9   Crockett, A. *Chudleigh*, p.32
10   Dymond and White, op.cit., p.9
11   Brixey, op.cit., p.69 (quoting State Papers Dom.)
12   Trotter, T. op.cit., 2nd.ed., 3v., 1804
13   Russell, op.cit., pp.49–51
14   White, J.T. *Torquay*, p.175
15   Brixey, pp.60–1
16   Trotter, op.cit., v.3, p.95
17   Torquay Directory, 31 July, 1912
18   Wilson, G. *The Old Telegraphs*, 1976
19   Brixey, op.cit. p.76
20   Oppenheim, p.117
21   Devon Life, Nov.1984, pp.50–1
22   Devon and Cornwall Notes and Queries, v.15, p.202

Chapter VII   1   Fisher, H.S.L., ed. *Ports and shipping in the South–West*, pp.131–45
2   Oppenheim, op.cit., p.27
3   *Billing's Directory*, 1857, p.500
4   Horsley, J. *Short History of Brixham*, p.11
5   *Trans. Devon. Assoc.*, v.39, 1907, pp.168–9
6   Ellis, A.C. *Historical Survey of Torquay*, p.412

TALL SHIPS IN TORBAY

Chapter XIII   1 Seymour, D.J. *Torre Abbey*, p.82
     2 *Trans. Devon. Assoc.*, v.83, p.279
     3 *Dartmouth Chronicle*, 10 Feb. 1882
     4 *Torquay Directory*, 31 Jul. 1889
     5 ibid., 17 Feb. 1882
     6 ibid., 24 Jun. 1903
     7 *Victorian and Edwardian Devon from old photographs*, p.94
     8 Clark, E.F. *George Parker Bidder*, p.198
     9 *Torquay Directory*, 17th Feb. 1882
   10 *Trans. Devon. Assoc.* v.39, 1907, pp.170–1
   11 *Torquay Chronicle*, 13 Sep. 1853
   12 March, E.J. *Sailing Trawlers*, p.215
   13 Corin, J. *Provident*
   14 Horsley, J. *Short History of Brixham*, p.18
   15 *Guardian*, 17 Feb. 1984

Chapter IX   1 Larn, R. op.cit., p.99
     2 White, J. op.cit., p.257
     3 *Torquay Directory*, 17 Jan. 1866
     4 Farr, G. *Wreck and Rescue on the coast of Devon: the story of the South Devon Lifeboats*, pp.107–153
     5 Farr, ibid., pp.154–8

Chapter X   1 Original letter in Torquay Museum
     2 *Torquay Directory*, 23 July 1919
     3 Official List of Rewards, submitted to Parliament, 1921
     4 Russell, P. op.cit., p.195
     5 Brierley, G.H. *Torbay Regattas, 1813–1913*
     6 Ellis, Arthur C. *History of Brixham*, Unpublished ms in Torquay Museum
     7 *After the Battle*, No.44, 1984, pp.1–31
     8 Official Account; published by the *Times*, 1956
     9 Charlton, W. *Voyage of the Mayflower*

BIBLIOGRAPHY

The material in this book has been gathered together for the first time but the prime reference source has been M.Oppenheim's *Maritime History of Devon* published by the University of Exeter in 1968. This s originally written for the *Victoria County History of Devon* which was never published.

Books containing relevant material (and referred to by the author's name) and frequently consulted are:

Brixey, A. *Story of Torbay*, 1889 (Does not give sources of quotations but they are mainly from the Calendars of State Papers)
Burton, S.H. *The South Devon Coast*
Delderfield, E.R. *The Torbay Story*
Devon County Council *The Coastlines of Devon*
Dymond, R. & White, J.T. *A Chronological Record of Events Relating to Torquay and neighbourhood* (from 1050 to 1880 but continued annually in the *Torquay Directory* to about 1930.) This is an invaluable source of information on maritime (and other) events but rarely gives the sources of the material; after 1847 however the summary is taken directly from the newspaper.
Farr, G. *Wreck and Rescue on the South Devon Coast of Devon*, 1968
Larn, R. *Devon Shipwrecks*

General local histories often quoted (and also referred to only by author's name) are:

Blewitt, O. *Panorama of Torquay*, 1832
White, J.T. *History of Torquay*, 1878
Ellis, A.C. *Historical Survey of Torquay*, 1930
Russell, P. *Torquay*, 1960
Patterson, C.H. *History of Paignton*, 1953
Penwell, F.R. *Paignton in Six Reigns*, 1953
Gregory, C. *Brixham in Devonia*

Bibliographical guides to Torquay, Paignton and Brixham published by Torbay Borough Council.

It is always desirable to research original documents but because of the problems and cost of using the Public Record Office much use has been made of the Calendars of State Papers. The worksheet compiled by David Fisher and published by the Nautical History Society, South West Section has been of inestimable value. This lists all those published to 1983 and gives some locations.

DEVON RECORD OFFICE holds *Shipping Registers* among other relevant documents. Note DRO's leaflet on *Maritime History*.
NEWSPAPERS Maritime matters in South Devon are covered in the following:
    Trewman's Exeter Flying Post from 1768
    Torquay Directory from 1846
    Torquay Times from 1869
    Western Morning News from 1860
    Herald Express from 1925

Other newspapers (e.g. *Torquay Chronicle*), were in existence also at various times. A full list is given in the Finding List issued by the Devon History Society in 1975. This will soon be superseded by the Devon volume of the British Library's *Bibliography of British Newspapers*.

TALL SHIPS IN TORBAY

The *Burnet Morris Index* containing some two million entries is kept in Westcountry Studies Library in Exeter and must be consulted by all local historians whatever their field of interest.

The Spanish Ship in Torbay (Chapter 2)
Overlapping accounts appear in:
    Brixey, pp.38—40
    Ellis, pp.123—130

Record of the Armada in Devon in *Notes and Gleanings* May 1888, pp.74—80 & June 1888, pp.81—85
    Russell, pp.30—1
    White, pp.42—63

IMPORTANT DATES IN TORBAY'S HISTORY

1001	Danes in South Devon; villages burned
1317	Torre Abbey granted rights to draw nets at Cockington
1338	Black Prince granted Water of Dartmouth including Torbay
1512	Ships pressed for navy service, Brixham, Paignton, etc.
1540	"Bulwarks" proposed at Berry Head, Beacon Hill, & elsewhere
c.1560	Dunkirkers (privateers from Europe) in Torbay
1588	Spanish Armada ship in Torbay. Prisoners in Tithe Barn
c.1590	Start of the Newfoundland fisheries
1623	John Nutt the pirate, taken by Sir John Eliot in Torbay
1626	King's Fleet "lies in Torbay much in need or cordage and sails"
1629	Pirates still in Torbay, including the notorious Downe
c.1650	Press Gang said to be hard at work in Devon
1664—7	Naval engagements against French & Dutch; de Ruyter in Bay
1688	William, Prince of Orange, landed at Brixham
1690	French fleet under Admiral Tourville in Torbay
1699	Plan from Mr Robinson for a proposed harbour or mould across the Bay
1727	Smugglers' boat brought into Torquay with arrack and tea
1740	Peter White "flogged through the fleet" for desertion
1771	Brig *St Peter* wrecked near Torre Abbey; wreckers caught
1778	Press Gang still at work. Torquay fisherman killed
1784	Convict ship in Torbay; prisoners escape and swim to Paignton
1787	Guernsey lugger lost in the Bay; crew of five drowned
1795	Great Storm; Earl Howe's fleet in great danger
c.1796	Hospital ship in Bay for "the sick of the fleet"
1800	Naval hospital set up at Goodrington
1803	New pier at Torquay; protection from Press Gang offered
1804	*Venerable* wrecked at Paignton
1805	Battle of Trafalgar; Fleet activity subsequently reduced
1811	Sailing match for open boats at Torquay (later the Regatta)
1815	Napoleon on board the *Bellerophon* in Torbay
1822	Coastguard Service established (station at Babbacombe 1825)

*c.*1830	Steamship *Brunswick* bringing visitors by sea
1838	Paignton Harbour Act passed (first vessels docked 1839)
1842	120 tubs of smuggled spirits found at Babbacombe
1843	Foundation stone of Brixham breakwater laid (completed 1916)
1845–60	Emigration from Torquay in Crossman's vessels
1850	90 tubs of smuggled spirits found at Babbcombe
1855	Last vessel launched at Shaw's Shipyard, Torquay
1859	Storm caused great damage in South Devon; vessels washed off stocks at Brixham shipyards
1866	Great hurricane in January; ships wrecked and many lives lost. *City of Exeter*, first Brixham lifeboat arrived
1868–9	"Duchy Dues" case; toll of 6d per ton agreed in lieu of dues in 1870
1870	Haldon Pier completed
1873	Wallace on fire; burnt out and a total loss
1876	Torquay Lifeboat arrived
*c.*1880	The larger ketch–rigged trawlers introduced at Brixham
1883	Emigrant ship left for Australia with 30 passengers
1890	Foundation stone for Princess Gardens and Pier laid
1902	Letters BM introduced for Brixham fishing boats
1910	Fleet Review in July by King George V. Graham White flew over ships to prove the aeroplane as a fighting weapon
1912	Large fleet in Torbay; visited by Winston Churchill
1913	Centenary of Torquay Regatta
1914–18	European War; RNAS seaplane base at Paignton
1920	Ex–German torpedo boats aground at Paignton
1923	Torquay lifeboat station closed
1936	Last appearance of the great "J" class yachts in Torbay
1939–45	World War II. Beaches mined and barbed–wire defences put up. Gun batteries at Brixham and Torquay
1944	United States forces left Torbay (and elsewhere) for beaches of Normandy
1948	Olympic yachting events held in Torbay
1956	Torquay to Lisbon Sail–Training Race took place *Mayflower II* launched from Upham's Shipyard, Brixham
1969	Review of the Fleet by HM the Queen
1971	New fish market and jetty opened at Brixham
1984	New marina opened at Torquay

INDEX

TALL SHIPS IN TORBAY

More books from Ex Libris Press are described on the following pages:

WEST COUNTRY TOUR
John Skinner
Edited and Introduced by Roger Jones

John Skinner is known to some as the author of diaries recording his life and thought as Rector of Camerton in the Somerset Coalfield and as an energetic amateur archaeologist.

Skinner undertook a tour of the West of England in 1797, at the age of 25 and before he found his role in life. In this previously unpublished manuscript we find a young man with a great curiosity to understand and record all he sees during his two months in Somerset, Devon and Cornwall. The resulting diary throws much light on the time when it was written.

Here is social history, topography and autobiography all rolled into one delightful mix.

'What makes John Skinner's diary of an excursion through Somerset, Devon and Cornwall in 1797 so notable, is its direct and uncluttered style: it will be of interest to layman and historian alike.'

James Mildren, *Western Morning News*

96 pages; 2 colour cover; 19 engravings and map
ISBN 0 950563 9 9   Price £2.95

GREEN ROAD TO LAND'S END
Roger Jones
Illustrated by Edward Dowden

On May Day 1984 Roger Jones set out to fulfil a modest but long held ambition to walk from London to Land's End. The author of several books for ramblers, he felt confident that he could cover the 400 or so miles in around three weeks.

He was soon to discover, however, that the five or six mile rambles to which he was accustomed had not prepared him for the rigours of this long-distance walk. The first day's 26 miles left him not only footsore but almost unable to put one foot in front of the other.

After six days he arrived at Avebury in Wiltshire, called his wife and took two days rest at home in Bradford on Avon. One new pair of walking boots and a visit to the hospital later, he started out once more and happily completed his route to the far west of England. 144 pages; full colour cover; 16 pen and ink drawings

ISBN 0 948578 01 7   Price £2.95

The above books may be obtained from your local bookshop or from the publisher, post-free, at 1 The Shambles, Bradford on Avon, Wiltshire.

A current list of titles will be sent upon request.